<u>BLACK AMERICA SERIES</u>

GREENE COUNTY
GEORGIA

Respectfully,
Mamie L. Hillman

BLACK AMERICA SERIES

GREENE COUNTY
GEORGIA

Mamie Lee Hillman

ARCADIA

ISBN 0-7385-1607-4

Published by Arcadia Publishing
an imprint of Tempus Publishing Inc.
Charleston SC, Chicago, Portsmouth NH, San Francisco

Printed in Great Britain

Library of Congress Catalog Card Number: 2003114006

For all general information contact Arcadia Publishing at:
Telephone 843-853-2070
Fax 843-853-0044
E-mail sales@arcadiapublishing.com
For customer service and orders:
Toll-Free 1-888-313-2665

Visit us on the internet at http://www.arcadiapublishing.com

CONTENTS

ACKNOWLEDGMENTS

I am so very grateful to the Lord for the opportunity to document some of Greene County's African-American history. I am truly indebted to Him for all things. I am grateful for all those persons who have gone before me and have given all that the Lord presented to them, and for those persons who poured their energies out to their families, their community, and its people; each of them was a part of the solution that addressed the challenges and dialogue of the day. These were men and women who oftentimes sacrificed themselves for the greater good of their families, because they discovered a higher vision and a calling that was not of man. These people were instruments of God. Today, we rejoice in the Lord for them, and we will not forget their contributions.

This book is lovingly dedicated to my family: my grandparents, John and Mamie Champion and Henry and Amy Akars; my wonderful parents, Reid and Ella Mae Champion; my husband, John L. Hillman Sr.; our spiffy children, Je'ohne, Lea, Bobby Jr., Julian, Ariza, and John Jr; and our grandchildren Bobby, Brianna, Daniel, and my granddaughter who is to be born in April 2004.

Lovingly submitted, Mamie

INTRODUCTION

Greene County, Georgia, was organized on February 3, 1786, and named for Revolutionary general Nathaniel Greene. Greensboro was named the county seat in 1803. The Creek Indians had inhabited Greene County since the early 1700s, living along the Oconee and Ogeechee Rivers. They were a very spirited, proud, and brave race of people.

As early as June 1735, a petition was sent to the Trustees of Georgia requesting that the use of black slaves be permitted, but their request was promptly refused. In December 1738 another request was sent to the Trustees again requesting permission to use slaves with proper limitations, but the request was denied. The Trustees of the Colony of Georgia would not even allow slaves to be hired from South Carolina. However, those who desired to use slave labor in Georgia continued their petitions. James Habersham, who supported the prohibition of slavery, stated that he once "thought that it was unlawful to keep negro slaves, but [that he] was induced to think God may have a higher end in permitting them to be brought to this Christian country, than merely to support their masters." Rev. George Whitfield, who also had first opposed slave labor, became convinced that it was necessary for the existence of the colony, and that it was really a Christian act to bring Africans to America and convert and civilize them. These men and others exerted influence in favor of the petitions being granted, although the Trustees of Georgia continued firm in their refusal.

On October 26, 1749, a convention of the colonists was called, for the Trustees became convinced that they must yield. The Trustees of Georgia approved the petition requesting that slavery be allowed at once under the proposed conditions. These conditions were as follows: the colonists employ one white male servant for every four male slaves; they should teach slaves no trade that would interfere with white citizens; inhumane treatment would be prevented; and moral and religious instructions should be given to them. A condition added by the convention was that a penalty of 10 pounds should be paid by every master who forced or permitted a slave to work on the Lord's Day, and that if he failed to compel his slave to attend church at some time on Sunday, he should be fined five pounds for each offense.

In 1825 there were 7,537 slaves, 128 free persons of color, and 5,952 whites in Greene County. Free persons of color date back in Greene County to 1819. There are no records in existence in Greene County that provide evidence of slave importation or list the slave and their origin. There is some census data, which provides us with names of the slaves, their plantation owners, the monetary value of the slave, their job description, and the time the census was taken. Greene County planters controlled the land, the slave laborers, and the politics. Slave labor was very profitable because of the cotton industry in Georgia. During this era in our history the planters were the powerful and the slave laborers were the powerless. The hideous yoke of slavery was the economic wealth that men were measured by. A slave could be maintained for less than $50 per year while bringing to the planters more than $300 to $500 in marketable goods (per slave). Dosia Harris, a slave who lived on a plantation near the town of Penfield, summarized her day as a slave by saying that "you work from sun up to sun down; you eat supper and fling yourself on the bed and go right to sleep."

Slavery hurt the spirit, soul, and body of the person who had to bear the burden of it. Countless men, women, and children experienced this, and remnants of this experience remain today in our culture.

The Emancipation Proclamation was issued by President Abraham Lincoln in January of 1863, and slavery ended in Georgia in June of 1865. This left many confused—the planters because their system of wealth ("king cotton") was dying, and the slaves because they did not fully understand what freedom meant and there were no productive resources available to them to assist them through this transition. During these times two of our oldest African-American churches were established: St. Paul Baptist Baptist Church (Woodville community) and Springfield Baptist Church (Canaan community). We as a people would have suffered a greater tragedy from the slave experience if it were not for the organizing of the churches throughout Greene County. Although our history in this place has been long and hard, it has been productive, for our forbears relied on their faith in God.

Change has continued in Greene County from the Reconstruction Act in 1867 through the present today. Several programs and agencies were established to assist individuals in the transition from slave laborers to citizens. Many of these programs and agencies failed and people continued to suffer.

Throughout the journey of African Americans in Greene County, we have contributed to the growth and betterment of this community. We are standing on the shoulders of those who have gone before us. We are living in the day that Abraham Colby, A.T. Chisolm, Rev. Levi Thornton, Rev. C.C. English, Sissy Barnhart, Rev. H.H. Hughes, and other notable women and men hoped for. We must never become complacent or take lightly the contributions that any of those who have gone on before us accomplished. They went beyond their circumstances, beyond the times in which they lived, and beyond the challenges of their daily lives.

This is only a small representation of the experiences of Greene County African-Americans. It is vital that we continue to research, document, disseminate, and preserve our history. This is our responsibility, for it is our legacy.

One
OUR FOREBEARS

The knowledge of our parents, grandparents, and other forbears blesses our hearts daily. Their accomplishments, their strengths in spite of their experiences, their courage to continue on, and their faith in the hope of a better day serve as a source of encouragement. Understanding the challenges they faced throughout their lives increases our love and respect for these individuals.

History touches our lives daily. It is important that we embrace it, reflect upon it, learn from it, and actively work not to repeat the atrocities from our past. This will build a greater future for our sons and daughters and the entire community.

We suffer greatly in society when our vices are exploited and our virtues are suppressed. The men and women presented here experienced much more than we could ever imagine. They did not have many earthly goods; they worked from sun-up until sundown, often under prejudicial employers; and yet they remained convinced that a better day was coming.

What are we doing with this day of opportunity? Have we resolved to rest on our laurels and become complacent? We are living in the day they hoped for and we should rejoice in the Lord for each of the people who have gone before us. It is our continued hope that each of us will become leaders in our homes, our churches, and our community. Greene County has given birth to some of the world's great men and women. They have and continue to make a difference in each of our lives.

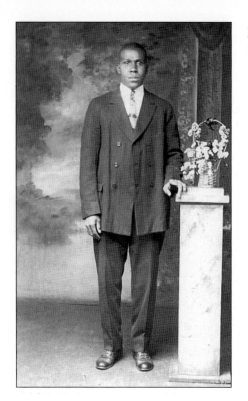

Hopp Butts is pictured, c. December 25, 1927. (Courtesy of the Butts Family.)

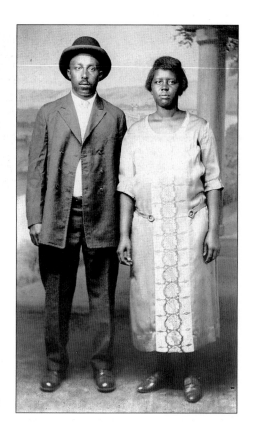

Shown here are Mr. and Mrs. Julius Butts, c. August 2, 1925. (Courtesy of the Butts Family.)

Clinton Butts is pictured, *c*. May 9, 1925.
(Courtesy of the Butts Family.)

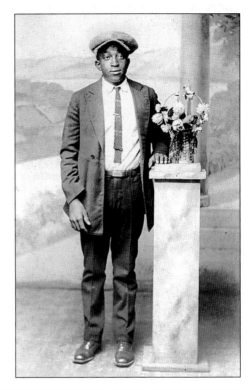

High school students at Antioch Church
School in Greensboro, Georgia, are
pictured in the mid–1940s. (Courtesy of
Danny Fullerton.)

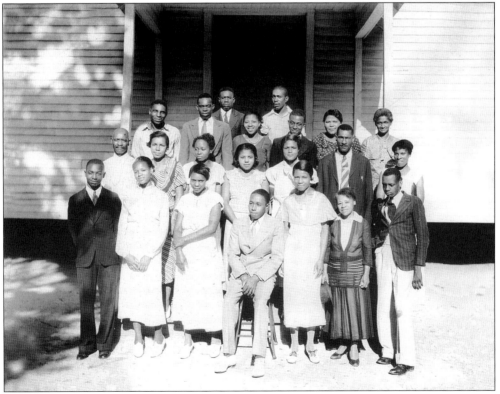

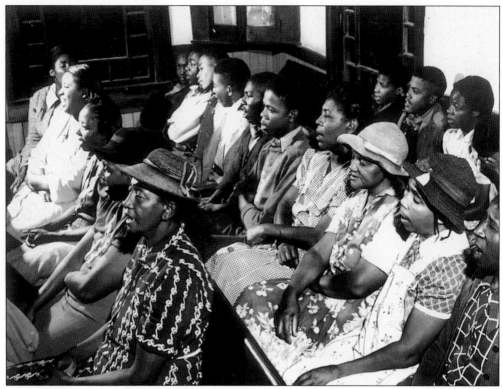

St. Paul Baptist Church in Woodville, Georgia, was organized in 1852. The congregation is pictured above. (Courtesy of Arthur Raper Collection, Chapel Hill, North Carolina.)

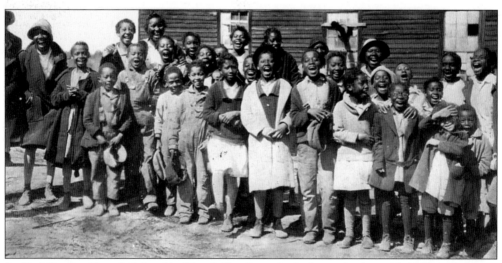

St. Paul Baptist Church School in Woodville, Georgia, is shown in the mid–1920s. (Courtesy of Arthur Raper Collection, Chapel Hill, North Carolina.)

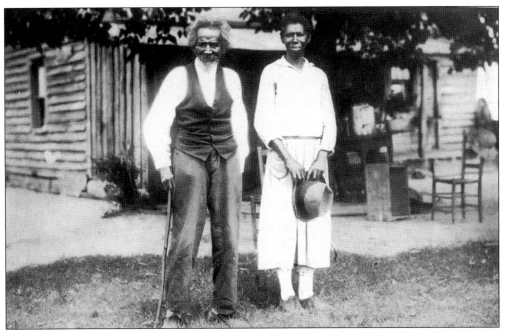

Jack and Sissy Barnhart of Greene County are pictured in the early 1900s. (Courtesy of Arthur Raper Collection, Chapel Hill, North Carolina.)

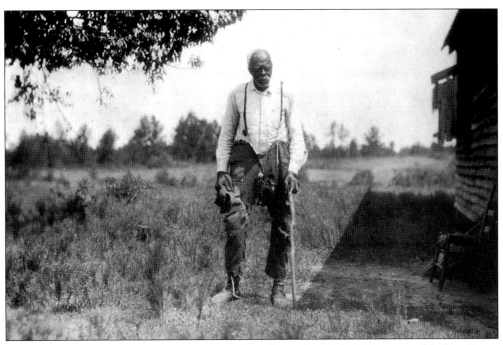

George Roach of Greene County is pictured in the early 1900s. (Courtesy of Arthur Raper Collection, Chapel Hill, North Carolina.)

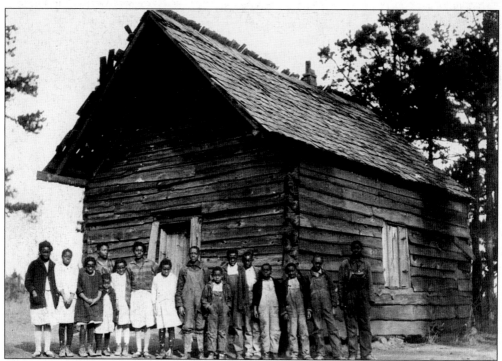

This early 1900s photograph presents Smith Chapel School students in Greene County, Georgia. (Courtesy of Arthur Raper Collection, Chapel Hill, North Carolina.)

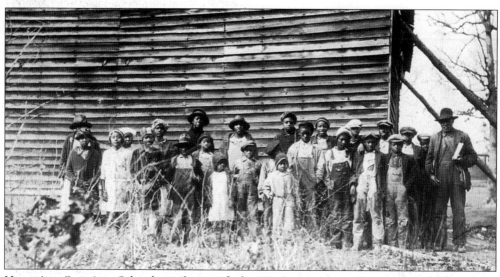

Mosquito Crossing School students of the Veazey community in Greensboro pose for a picture in the early 1800s. (Courtesy of Arthur Raper Collection, Chapel Hill, North Carolina.)

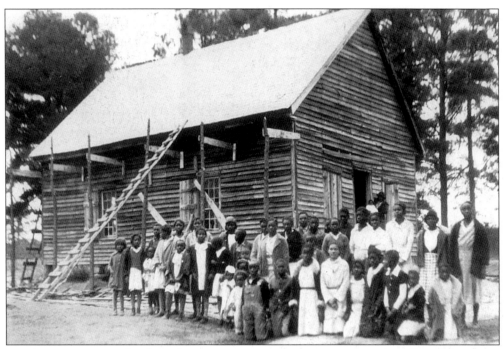

Hutchinson Grove School students in Greene County are pictured in the early 1900s. (Courtesy of Arthur Raper Collection, Chapel Hill, North Carolina.)

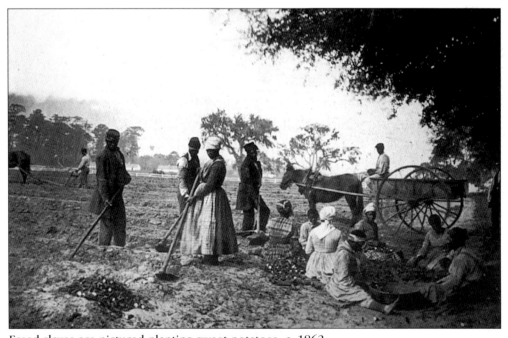

Freed slaves are pictured planting sweet potatoes, *c.* 1862.

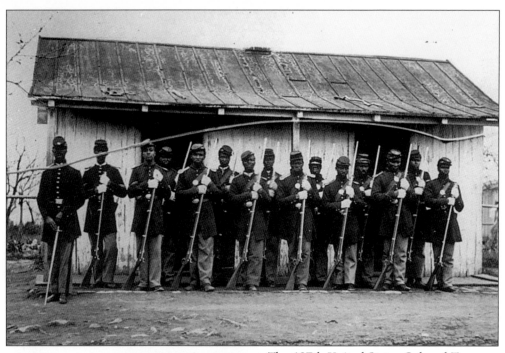

The 107th United States Colored Troops, pictured above, were assigned to guard the United States Capitol in Washington, D.C., in 1865.

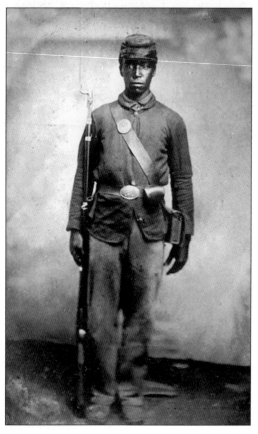

This 1863 recruiting poster proclaims, "Men of Color, To Arm! Now or Never."

Two
FAITH

Green County's African-American churches are arguably one of the greatest institutions that African Americans have created. Churches have held together more African Americans than any other organization or agency, and they have had the greatest influence on molding and shaping our thoughts and lives.

The history of faith is interwoven in the African-American experience. Just as human slavery is a part of history, so is faith. If it were not for the African-American churches, African Americans would have suffered even more deeply during times of slavery. Regardless of the hideous slave status, African Americans aspired to love and hope and exemplified this from sun-up until sun-down. Therefore, the African-American church is the ineradicable witness of our spiritual greatness through Jesus Christ.

The majority of African-American churches throughout Greene County were formed after the Emancipation Proclamation. Before the proclamation African Americans were not permitted to form their own churches and their forebears were only allowed to sit in the balconies or rear pews of our sister white churches. Those great church pioneers experienced the struggle, the strain, and the separatism first-hand as slaves. They longed to create a space where an impartial system could be established that would affirm their human dignity. Thus, they longed to experience true worship.

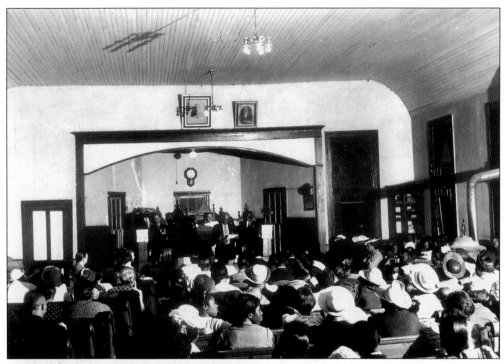

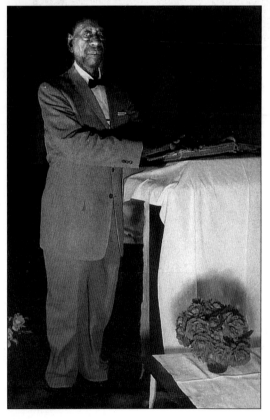

The Siloam Missionary Baptist Church congregation is pictured above. Siloam Missionary, in Union Point, Georgia, was organized in 1867. This congregation had its beginning in the (white) Bethesda Baptist Church. In 1866, 38 African Americans began the process of organizing their own church. (Courtesy of Arthur Raper Collection, Chapel Hill, North Carolina.)

Rev. H.H. Hughes was the first pastor of the Hill Chapel Baptist Church in Greensboro. Hill Chapel was organized in 1938. Reverend Hughes and his wife are buried behind the church. (Courtesy of the Hill Chapel Baptist Church.)

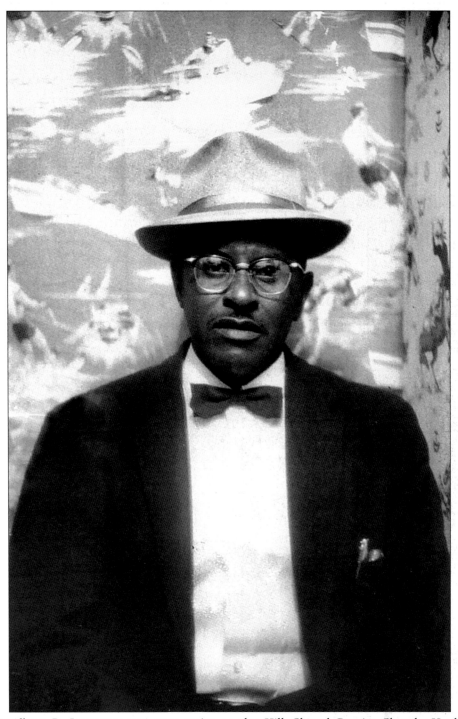

Rev. Albert B. Lawrence was very active at the Hill Chapel Baptist Church. He later became pastor of Mt. Zion Baptist Church in Hancock County, Georgia. (Courtesy of Mrs. Claudia Lawrence.)

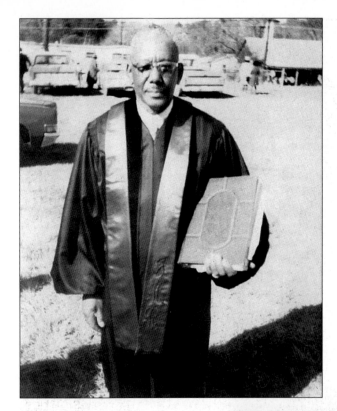

Rev. J.H. Russell was the second pastor of the Hill Chapel Baptist Church. He was a native of Covington, Georgia. (Courtesy of the Hill Chapel Baptist Church.)

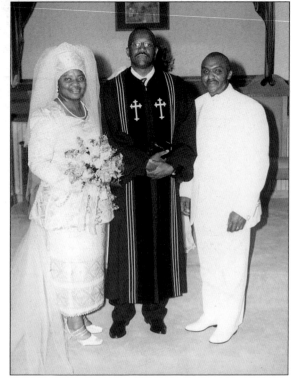

Rev. Herman Laguines is the fourth pastor of the Hill Chapel Baptist. In this photograph, he is officiating at the 25th wedding celebration of John and Mamie Hillman. He still serves as pastor of the Hill Chapel Baptist Church. (Courtesy of John and Mamie Hillman.)

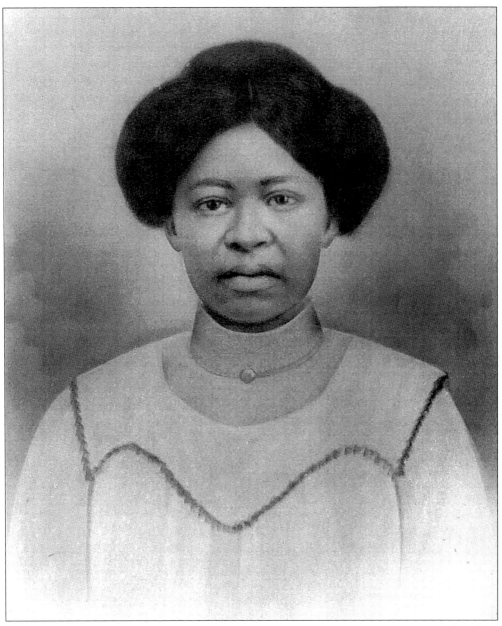

Fannie Roach Webb was a member of County Line African Methodist Episcopal Church in the Veazey community. (Courtesy of Ruby Jackson.)

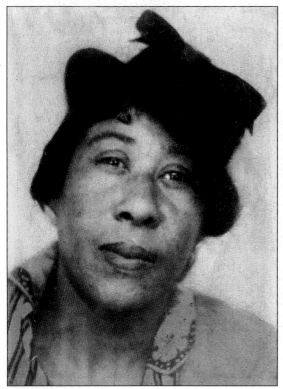

Lula Webb Raper was a member of the Hill Chapel Baptist Church in Greensboro, Georgia. She served on the Mother Board at the church. The Mother Board of Churches at that timed served many purposes. They were instrumental in preparing the sacraments for the Lord's Supper. They performed duties as pastor aides and other church needs, as well. However, their main purpose was to tutor young women in their spiritual growth as Christian women. (Courtesy of Ruby Jackson.)

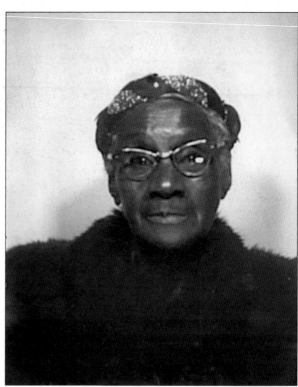

Mary S. Moore was a member of Second Baptist Church in White Plains, Georgia. (Courtesy of Mamie Hillman.)

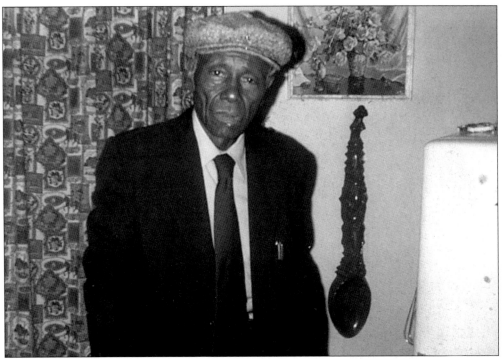

Joseph Fambro was a steward at the Ebenezer African Methodist Church in Greensboro. He operated the local shoe shop in downtown Greensboro for years. (Courtesy of the late Mary Fambro.)

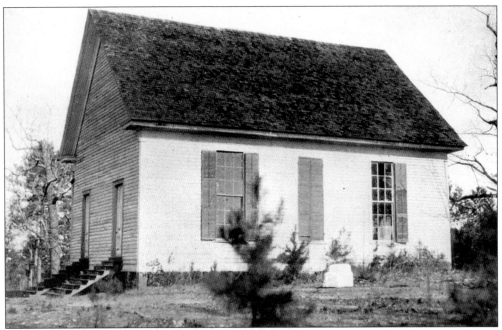

Emmanuel Baptist Church in Greene County is pictured in the late 1800s. This church is no longer in existence. (Courtesy of Arthur Raper Collection, Chapel Hill, North Carolina.)

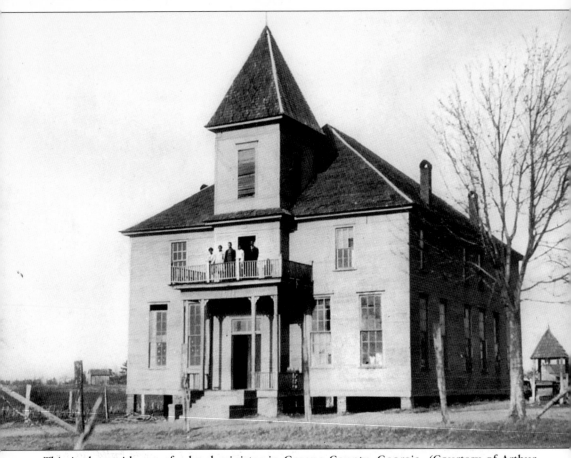

This is the residence of a local minister in Greene County, Georgia. (Courtesy of Arthur Raper Collection, Chapel Hill, North Carolina.)

Three
CHURCH SCHOOLS

In 1872, the Georgia legislature authorized that all counties establish public schools for all children. In Greene County there were two to three schools in each militia district. There were two boards of trustees—one for African Americans and one for whites. African-American schools were housed in lodges, church buildings, and in some buildings that were erected next to the churches. The majority of these schools were unfit for human use. Nevertheless, the teachers used what was given to them, because they knew the value of educating the children. The churches and neighborhoods surrounding the schools supported them as much as they could. The trustees and teachers served tirelessly to continue beyond this great stepping stone for African Americans, for education was the road that led to the betterment of their sons and daughters. The communities of Greene County certainly rejoice in the Lord for the support of our local churches for their vision and commitment toward education.

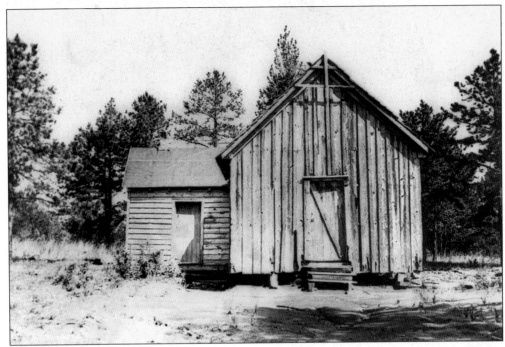

Public Square School was built before 1910. (Courtesy of the Greene County African-American Museum Archives.)

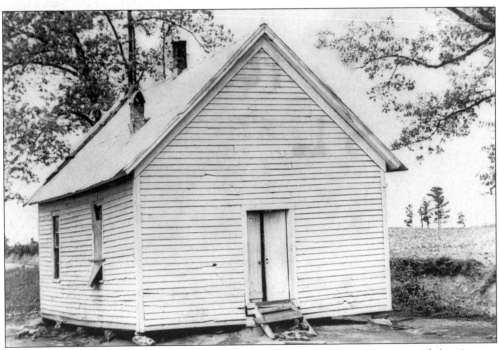

Mt. Pleasant School in Union Point, Georgia, is pictured above. (Courtesy of the Greene County African-American Museum Archives.)

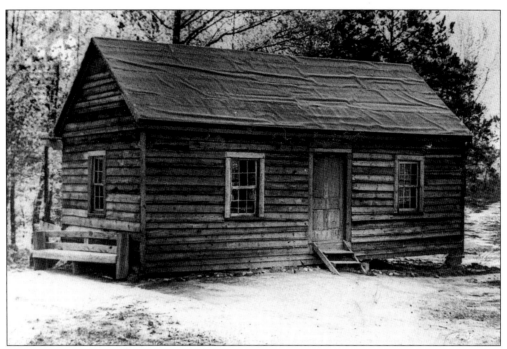

Shown here is Boswell Chapel School in Greensboro, Georgia. (Courtesy of the Greene County African-American Museum Archives.)

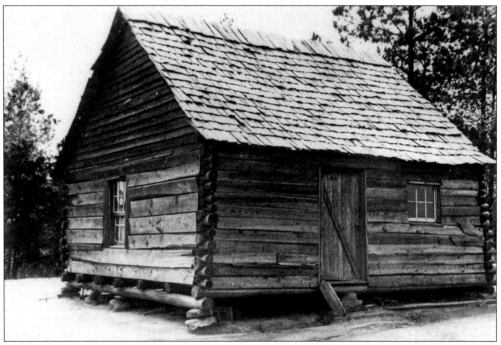

Smith Chapel School was located in the Liberty community of Greensboro, Georgia. (Courtesy of the Greene County African-American Museum Archives.)

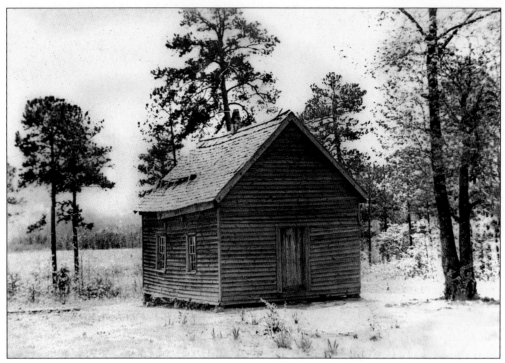

Hutchinson Grove School in Greensboro, Georgia, is pictured above. (Courtesy of the Greene County African-American Museum Archives.)

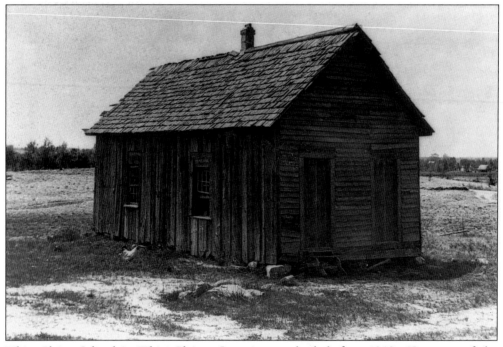

White Plains School in White Plains, Georgia, was built before 1910. (Courtesy of the Greene County African-American Museum Archives.)

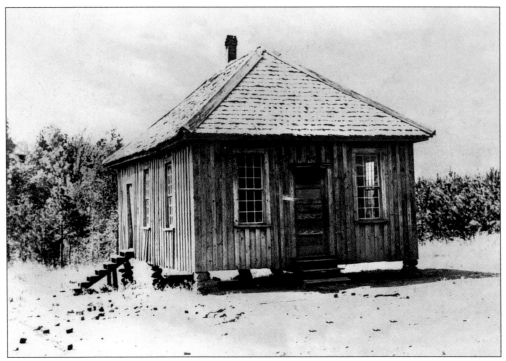

Randolph School in Union Point, Georgia, was built before 1910. (Courtesy of the Greene County African-American Museum Archives.)

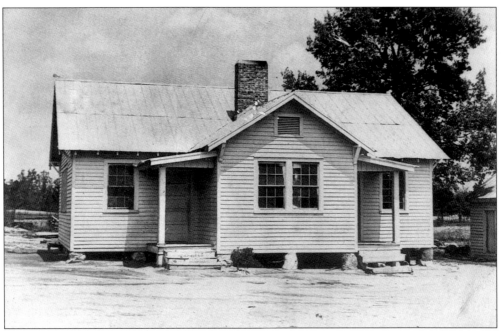

Eastover School in White Plains, Georgia, is pictured above. Rev. C.C. English, an educator, was actively involved in this school as well as the entire Eastover community. (Courtesy of the Greene County African-American Museum Archives.)

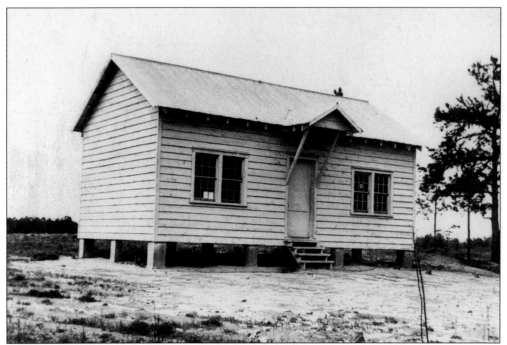

County Line School was located in White Plains, Georgia. (Courtesy of the Greene County African-American Museum Archives.)

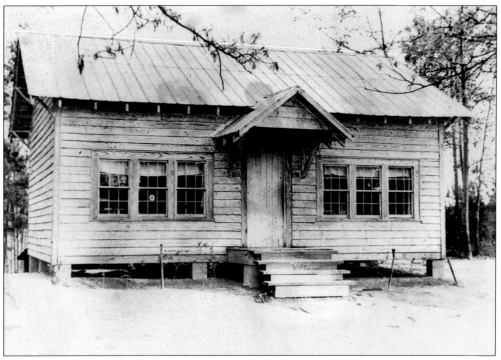

Springfield School, located in Greensboro, Georgia, is pictured above. (Courtesy of the Greene County African-American Museum Archives.)

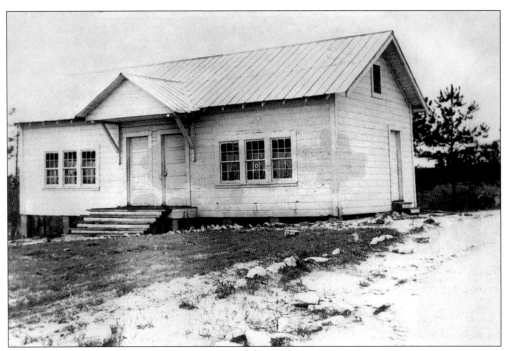

Shown here is Mosquito Crossing in White Plains, Georgia. (Courtesy of the Greene County African-American Museum Archives.)

Mrs. Julia Williams's fifth grade class at the Hubert English Elementary School in Siloam, Georgia, is pictured here. The Hubert English School building has become dilapidated through the years, because it is no longer in use. (Courtesy of the Greene County African-American Museum Archives.)

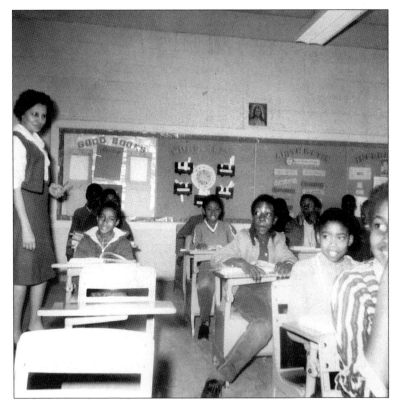

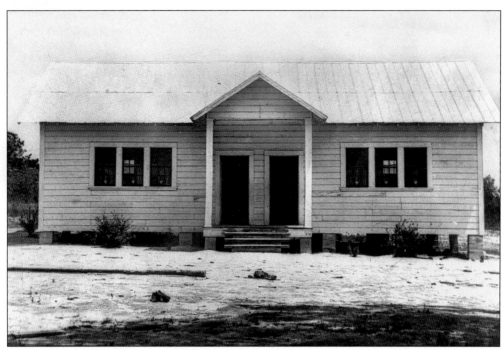

Rock Hill School was located in White Plains, Georgia. (Courtesy of the Greene County African-American Museum Archives.)

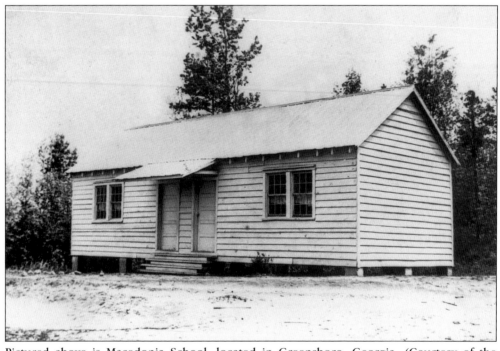

Pictured above is Macedonia School, located in Greensboro, Georgia. (Courtesy of the Greene County African-American Museum Archives.)

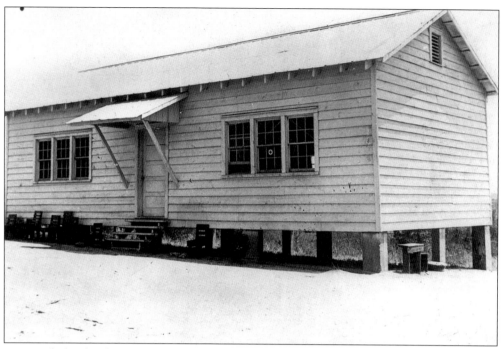

New Bethel School was located in Greensboro, Georgia. (Courtesy of the Greene County African-American Museum Archives.)

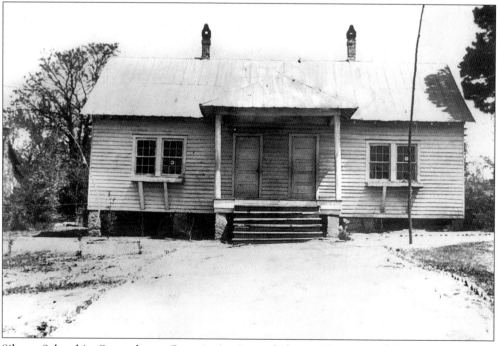

Siloam School in Greensboro, Georgia, is pictured above. (Courtesy of the Greene County African-American Museum Archives.)

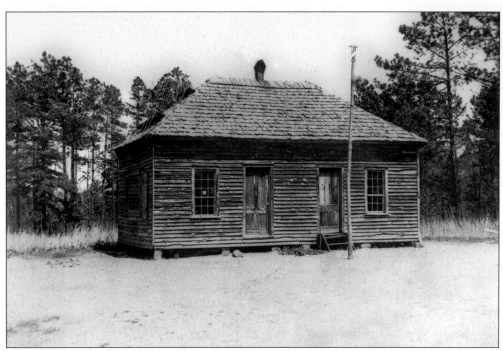

Shown here is Antioch School, located in Greensboro, Georgia. (Courtesy of the Greene County African-American Museum Archives.)

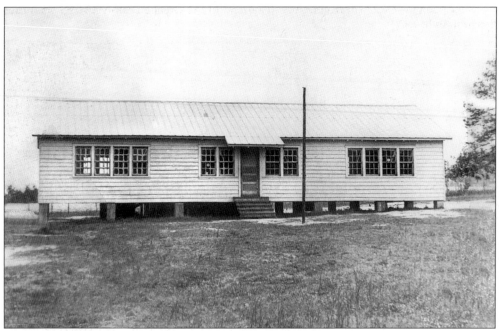

White Plains School in White Plains, Georgia, is pictured above. It was located below Second Baptist Church in the Pittsburg community in White Plains. This building was used for Greene County's first senior center. The building is no longer in existence, because it was destroyed by fire. (Courtesy of the Greene County African-American Museum Archives.)

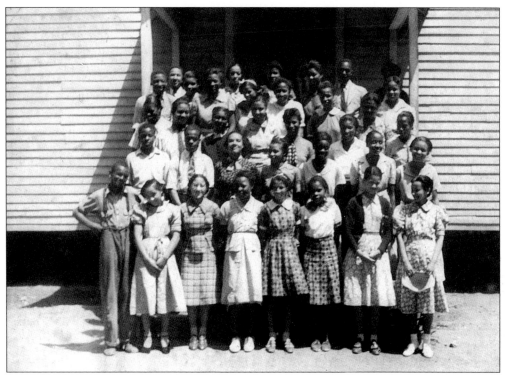

Pictured above is a Greensboro Normal and Industrial School class in Greensboro, Georgia. It was located in the Canaan community. (Courtesy of the Greene County African-American Museum Archives.)

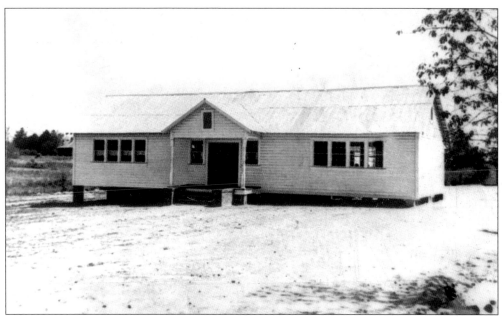

Union Point School in Union Point, Georgia, is pictured above. (Courtesy of the Greene County African-American Museum Archives.)

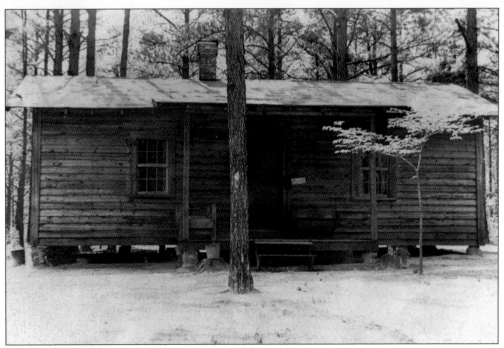

Shown here is Pine Grove School in Greensboro, Georgia. (Courtesy of the Greene County African-American Museum Archives.)

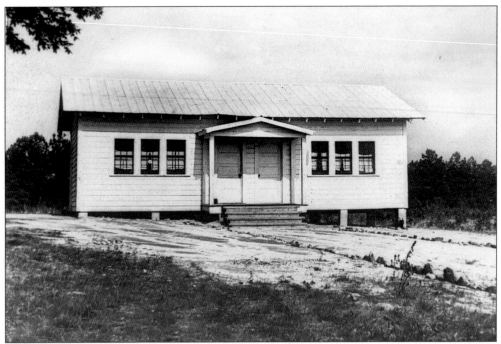

Bethelbera School was located in Greensboro, Georgia. (Courtesy of the Greene County African-American Museum Archives.)

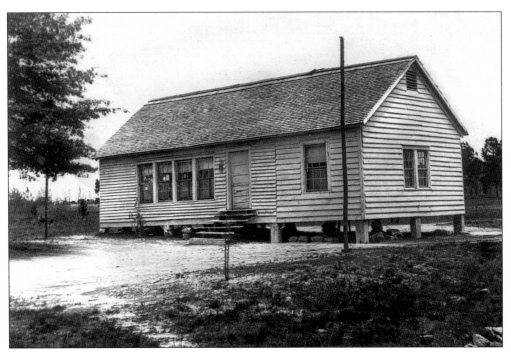

Andrews Chapel School in Greensboro, Georgia, is pictured above. (Courtesy of the Greene County African-American Museum Archives.)

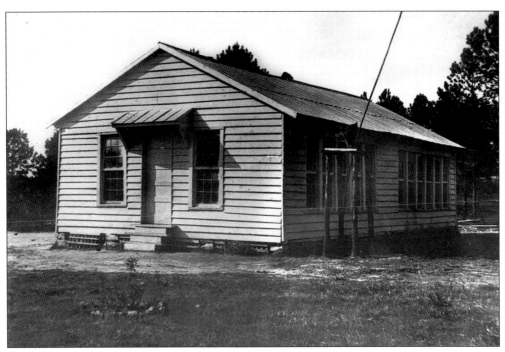

Shown here is Caldwell Chapel School in Greene County, Georgia. (Courtesy of the Greene County African-American Museum Archives.)

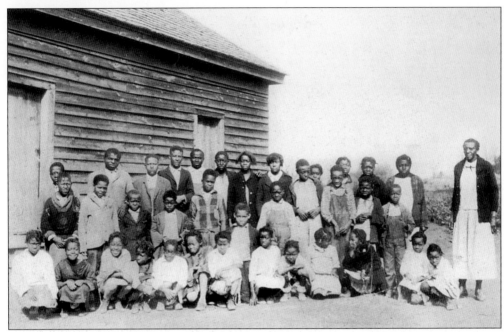

Flat Rock School was located in the Veazey community of Greensboro, Georgia. (Courtesy of the Greene County African-American Museum Archives.)

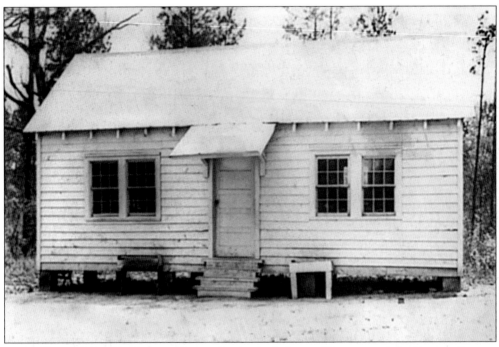

Jones Chapel School in Greene County is pictured above. (Courtesy of the Greene County African-American Museum Archives.)

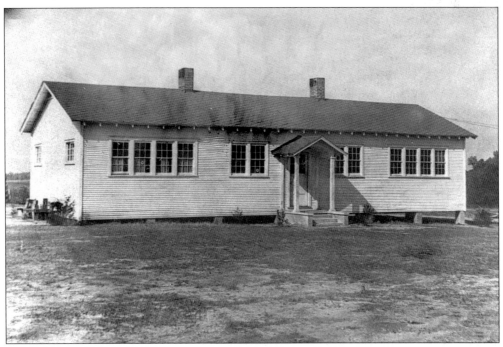

Shown above is Woodville School in Woodville, Georgia. (Courtesy of the Greene County African-American Museum Archives.)

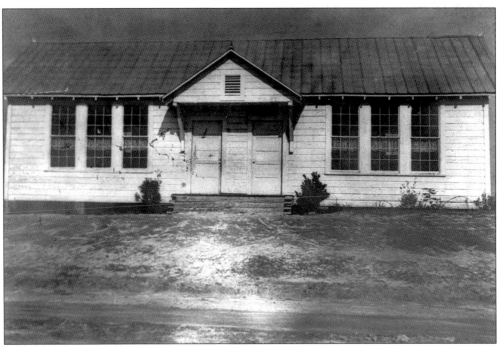

Penfield School was located in Penfield, Georgia. (Courtesy of the Greene County African-American Museum Archives.)

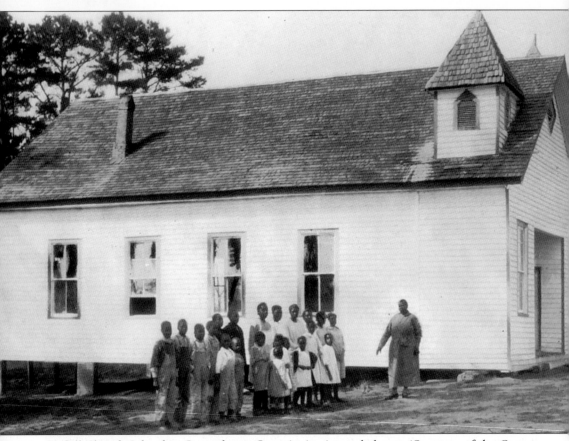

Bethel Church School in Greensboro, Georgia, is pictured above. (Courtesy of the Greene County African-American Museum Archives.)

Four
POLITICIANS

Greene County African Americans became active in politics in 1868. The majority of African Americans were voting for the Republican Party. Greene County was represented by a Republican candidate named Abraham Colby, who was a very popular candidate among his people.

Abraham Colby was born on the plantation of John Colby, a wealthy planter, in the Penfield community of Greene County in 1820. After John's wife died, he begat Abraham by his 16-year-old slave named Mary. Although reared under the hideous yoke of slavery, Abraham rose to greatness. He was a minister and a barber, and he became Greene County's first African-American representative to the Georgia General Assembly in 1868. Abraham Colby could not read or write; therefore, he took his son William with him to the assembly to handle those responsibilities.

In 1868, Abraham Colby and 32 other African-American representatives from around the state of Georgia went to the General Assembly. On September 5, 1868, these men were ousted from the Georgia General Assembly because of their color. The Georgia House Resolution 153, written on September 5, 1868, stated, "Whereas the House of Representatives of this State has recently decided after investigation of the subject and examination of the Constitution and laws of this State, that the persons of Color are ineligible as Members of this House, and thereby virtually declaring the ineligibility of persons of color to any and all offices of this State." On June 15, 1869, the Georgia Supreme Court ruled that African Americans were citizens and all citizens could hold office. On October 29, 1869, Klansmen invaded Colby's home in Greene County. They had previously tried to bribe him with $5,000 to vote in accordance with their beliefs; however, he refused. Therefore, they took him from his bed to some isolated woods and whipped him for three hours or more, leaving him for dead. Colby was very proud and truthful, and he was an effective leader in Greene County. We are very proud of his contributions, as well as others who served Greene County unselfishly when threats of death were presented.

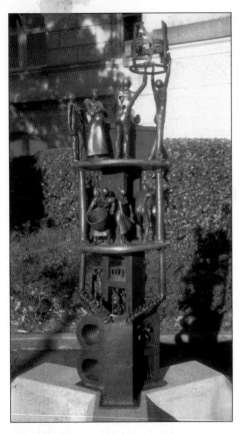

This six-foot, two-inch bronze statue entitled *Expelled Because of Color* was donated by the Black Caucus of the General Assembly in 1976 to commemorate the Bicentennial. Created by the late John Riddle Jr., a native Californian, the statue is a sensitive and powerful tribute to the 33 state legislators who were elected to the Georgia General Assembly and ousted almost immediately in 1868. The statue reads, "Although African-Americans had the right to vote and elect their own representatives in 1868, according to the 13th Amendment to the Constitution, there was no provision allowing African-Americans to hold office." The cinder block base at the bottom of the sculpture, flanked by the names of the 33 legislators, represents the foundation of African-American history. The story of the struggle unfolds in the above tiers.

The third of 16 children, Willie E. Chester Sr. was educated in Greene County public schools. He received his bachelor's degree in chemistry and natural science at Paine College and a master's degree in education and administration at Clark-Atlanta University and the University of Georgia. After a brief stint in the U.S. Army, he returned to Greene County and served as an educator for over 32 years. Chester was selected as Greene County's "Teacher of the Year" in 1968. He also served on the Greensboro City Council for 24 years and as mayor pro-tem of Greensboro for 14 years. He was the first African-American president of the Greene County Lions Club and was the founder and president of Chester Enterprises Inc. He was also the first African American to be appointed mayor of Greensboro, Georgia. (Courtesy of Mrs. Lenester Chester.)

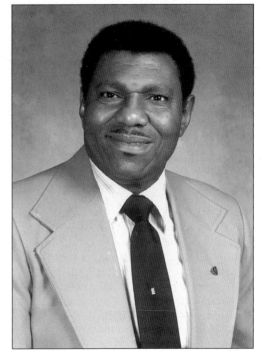

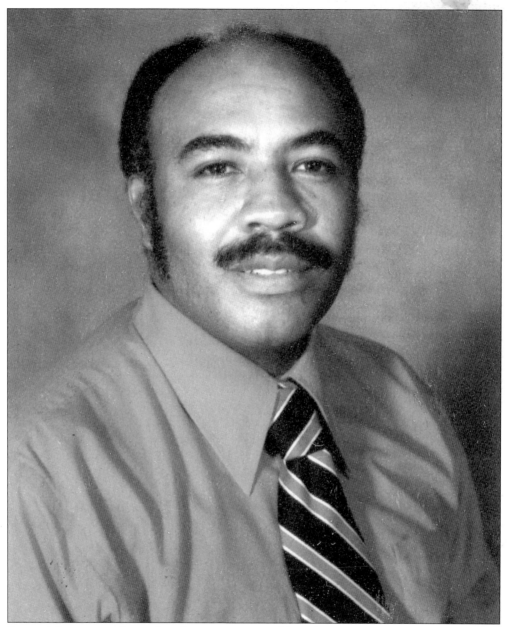

Benny Asbury was educated in Greene County public schools. Upon graduation from high school, he attended Morehouse College and Atlanta University. He engaged in additional studies at Savannah State College, Georgia College, and the University of Georgia. After serving in the U.S. Army, Asbury returned to Greene County to become an educator for 35 years. He became Greene County's first African-American official elected since 1868. He was elected to serve on the Union Point City Council for 12 years. Asbury was then elected to the Greene County Board of Commissioners, serving as vice-chair for almost 19 years. On April 20, 1999, Asbury was elected as chairman of the Greene County Board of Commissioners, making him the first African American to serve in this position. He served in this position until his death on September 14, 1999. (Courtesy of Mrs. Carol Asbury.)

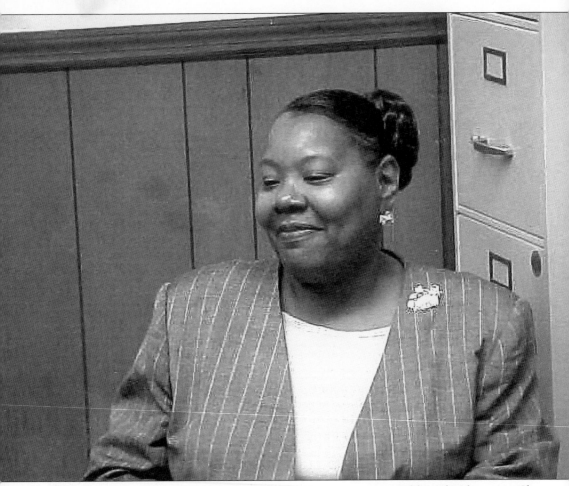

Deborah Smith received her education in the Greene County public school system. She attended Marsh-Draughon Business College in Atlanta, Athens Technical School in Athens, and Georgia Military College in Milledgeville, where she received her associate's degree. She is very active in many local organizations and has represented District 2 on the Greene County Board of Education since 1999. (Courtesy of Mrs. Deborah Smith.)

Five
EDUCATORS

Greene County schools have come a long way from the church schools that were in each militia district. At that time, many were not in a suitable shape to be used; however, they were the only ones available. These early educators often had to stuff rags in holes, nail boards and pieces of tin over cracks, and gather students around pot bellied stoves just to keep warm. Regardless of the poor condition of the schools, these educators were also committed to providing the opportunity of an education to Greene County students. The African-American schools improved slowly, and it wasn't until integration that supplies and earnings were finally equal. Teachers like those presented in this chapter are among the ones who helped the Greene County school system provide a quality education to all children, regardless of race, in the community.

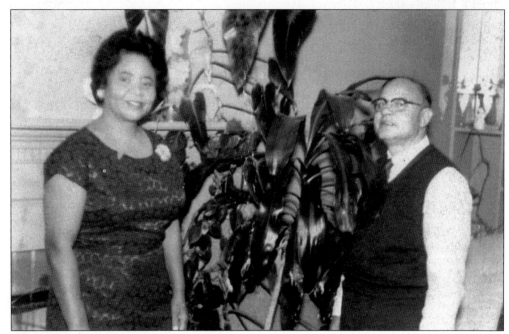

Eli Jackson was educated in Oglethorpe County public schools and attended Fort Valley State College, Tuskegee Institute, Atlanta University, and Temple University. Jackson became principal of Floyd Thomas Corry High School in 1951. In 1971, it was mandated that all public schools be integrated, and Jackson became assistant principal for Greene County High School, where he served until his retirement. He will always be remembered as a community leader that was an advocate for students, parents, and the entire community. He is seen with his greatest supporter, his wife. (Courtesy of Loretta Moon.)

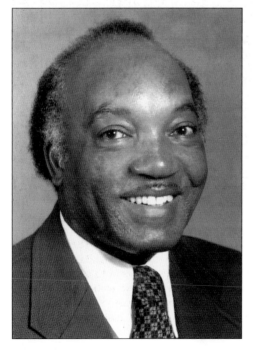

William J. Breeding Sr. was educated in the public schools of Birmingham. He earned his bachelor's degree from Clark College, his master's degree from Atlanta University, his sixth-year specialist degree from Atlanta University, and his post-graduate advanced study from the University of Georgia. Breeding came to Greene County in 1951. He has served the Greene County school system for over 40 years, both as educator and principal. (Courtesy of Mr. William J. Breeding Sr.)

46

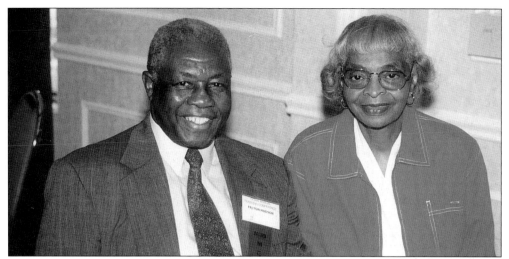

Felton Hudson was educated in Greene County public schools. He received his bachelor of arts degree from Morehouse College and his master's degree from the University of Georgia. Hudson served in the U.S. Air Force from 1951 to 1953. He has served as both educator and principal (Open Gate Alternative School). On November 7, 2000, Hudson was elected chairman of the Greene County Board of Education—the first African American to be elected in that position. He is photographed with his wife, Lucille Hudson. (Courtesy of Mr. Felton Hudson.)

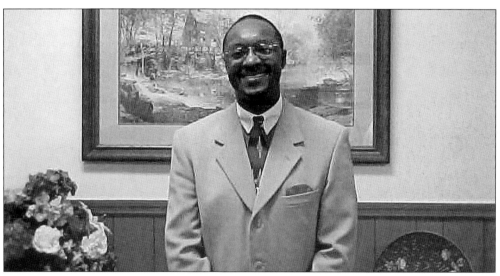

Rev. Joseph Nunnally is a native of Oconee County, Georgia, where he attended public school. He attended Georgia College in Milledgeville and graduated with a joint degree in social science and education. Reverend Nunnally has been working in Greene County since 1979. He began as a social studies teacher at the Greene-Taliaferro Comprehensive High School. In 1995, he became the first African-American principal at Greene-Taliaferro Middle School. Nunnally has been the administrative coordinator (an assistant superintendent position) of the Greene County school system since 2002. In addition to being employed by the Greene County school system, Reverend Nunnally serves as pastor of the Rock Hill Missionary Baptist Church in White Plains, Georgia. (Courtesy of Rev. Joseph Nunnally.)

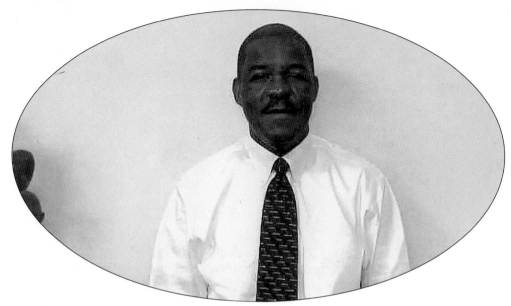

Dr. John Jackson is a native of Lake Charles, Louisiana, where he attended public school. He graduated from McNeese State University in 1977 with a degree in biology education. He began working in the local school system, teaching ninth grade science and high school chemistry. During this period he earned his masters and specialist degrees from McNeese in 1979 and 1982. In 1986, he earned his doctorate from Louisiana State University. All of his graduate degrees are in education administration and supervision. Currently Jackson serves as superintendent of the Greene County school system; he is the first African American to serve in this position. (Courtesy of Dr. John Jackson.)

Dedication Of Anita White Carson Middle School Draws Large Crowd

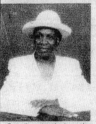

School Board Chairman Mike M Jones, Vice-Chair Anita W Carson, and members Yvonn Heidbrider, Deborah Smith, an Earl Engel. Mr. Jones introduce special guests and gave the his tory of the development of the ne middle school. He indicated that took a coalition of many groups i Greene County to make the Anit White Carson Middle School reality and gave utmost thanks t the citizens of Greene County wh supported the sales tax whic made it possible.

Over three hundred people attended the dedication of the Anita White Carson Middle School. County Commission Chairman Tim Bramlett, Commissioners Darrel Phelps, Marion Rhodes, and newly elected Commissioners Betty Jo Evans and Titus Andrews, and Senator Faye Smith were in attendance to recognize Mrs. Carson for her commitment to education and community and area improvement. The Chamber of Commerce was represented by Sid Lane. The SPLOST Oversight Committee Chairman Dick Sylte, and committee members Sam Gutherie and Sherley Selman were there to see the results of all their work. Members of the Special Committee for Better Education who helped pass the one cent sales tax, Co-chair Felton Hudson and William J. Breeding were there and Marvin Watson, Co-chair, sent his con-

The Wind Beneath My Wing was the theme of the recognitio program and Tyrone Eves gave beautiful rendition of the son Close friends of Mrs. Carson, fro childhood through college, throug sorority membership which contin ues to this day, made comment and gave gifts of appreciation fo her service and support. Maria Hatch, a friend from childhoo spoke of their lifelong friendshi and their work toward commo goals of improvement in man areas of society through thei sorority, Alpha Kappa Alph Helen Smith commented on th community service of Mrs. Carso Her uplifting guidance to he students, her children, and he friends was evident in the testi mony given by all. The William sisters, former students, brough gifts, a quilt symbolizing The Win Beneath My Wings, and Louis performed a dance, symbolizin Mrs. Carson's uplifting leadershi

Anita White Carson is a native of Rosedale, a small incorporated town in Jefferson County, Alabama. She received her formal education in the Jefferson County and Birmingham City school systems. After her high school graduation, she attended Clark College in Atlanta. She matriculated at Clark for freshman and sophomore credits and completed her undergraduate requirements at Miles College in Birmingham. Carson earned master's degrees in education and social work at the University of Georgia, Ohio Wesleyan, and Atlanta University. Additional studies were done at Grambling, Indiana, and A&T Universities. Carson taught 37 years in Greene County's educational system. She retired in 1990 and has since been active throughout the community volunteering her time. She was the first African-American woman to serve on the Greene County Board of Education. Carson has been presented countless honors and accolades in her lifetime; in 1999, Anita White Carson Middle School was named in her honor. (Courtesy of Mrs. Anita White Carson.)

Six

MEDICAL PIONEERS

Medical knowledge and technology has come a long way. In the beginning of Greene County there were no professional medical practices. The pioneers had to depend on home remedies that they had learned from their ancestors.

The first African-American physician arrived in Greene County in the very early 1900s. Dr. A.T. Chisolm was born in St. George, South Carolina, in 1880. His parents were Willie Chisolm and Mary (Felder) Chisolm. He married Claudia Byrd, a local girl, on July 4, 1912. Through this union, three daughters were born: Blanche, Thomasine, and Wila Bell. They resided in downtown Greensboro. Dr. Chisolm died of pneumonia on January 30, 1921, and is buried in the cemetery behind Springfield Baptist Church.

Dr. Calvin Melvin Baber became Greene County's second African-American physician in 1921. Dr. Baber was born on December 2, 1905, to Caleb Baber and Sallie (Banbridge) Baber. Dr. Baber grew up in Milstead, Alabama. He received his education at Talladega Secondary School and Talladega University from 1911 to 1916 in Talladega, Alabama. Dr. Baber received his medical degree from Meharry School of Medicine in Nashville, Tennessee. Dr. Baber was very active throughout the Greene County communities. He owned an office building in downtown Greensboro, which provided businessmen and women a space to provide their services to the community. Dorothy Brown's beauty salon, Dr. Baber's office, and many other businesses were all located there. Dr. Baber also assisted many families in acquiring better housing. He sponsored soft ball games throughout the summer, was active in real estate, and provided funds for the Ebenezer Episcopal Methodist Church to purchase land and build their parsonage in the 1920s.

Dr. Baber's residence at 1415 North East Street, Greensboro, Georgia, is on the National Registrar of Historical Places. In 1999, an initiative began to restore Dr. Baber's historical home; after restoration is completed, it will house the Greene County African-American Cultural Museum and Resource Center Inc. Dr. Baber died on November 22, 1945, of a cerebral hemorrhage. He is buried at the Pleasant Grove Cemetery in Bullock, Alabama.

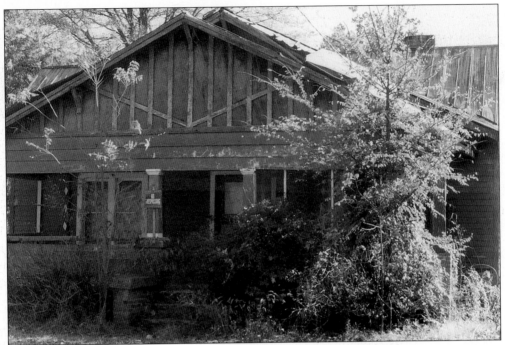

Dr. Calvin M. Baber's home became dilapidated due to natural elements and the lack of care by its previous owner. This photograph depicts the front of the house and its condition when the restoration initiative began in the fall of 1999. The house is a bungalow-style home built in 1921. (Courtesy of Greene County African-American Museum Archives.)

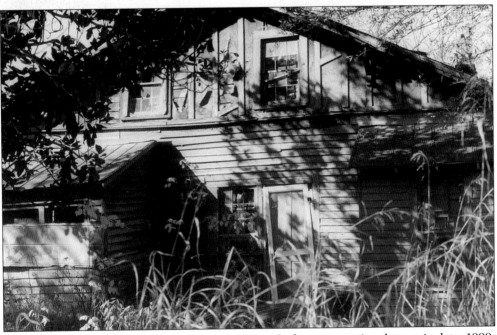

This is the rear of Dr. Calvin M. Baber's home before restoration began in late 1999. (Courtesy of Greene County African-American Museum Archives.)

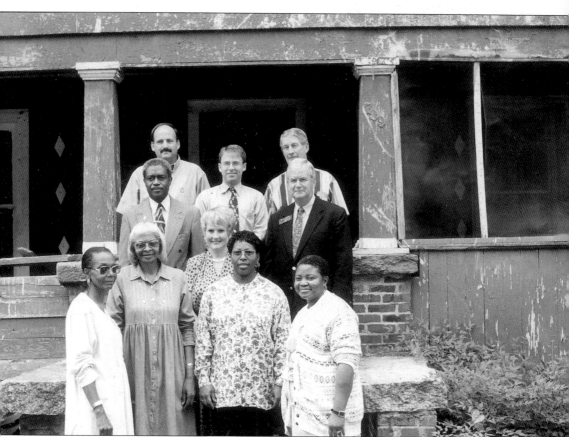

The Dr. Calvin M. Baber Historical Home Restoration Initiative and some of its supporters are pictured and include Mary L. Breeding, Lucille Hudson, Jackie Richardson, Lynn Hudson (Greene County Chamber of Commerce), Senator Griffin, Burt Walker (Northeast Regional Developmental Center), Rep. Mickey Channell, Raburn Neal (Georgia Power), and Jim Hunt (Chairman of Greene County Board of Commissioners). (Courtesy of Greene County African-American Museum Archives.)

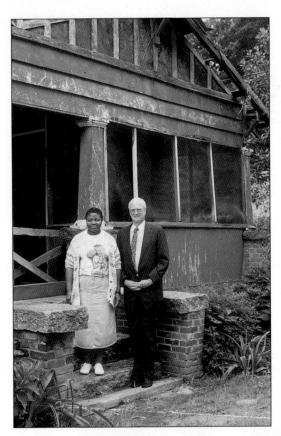

Mamie Hillman, the Dr. Calvin M. Baber Historical Home Restoration Initiative director, stands on the steps with Sibley Bryan, president of Chipman Union Manufacturing Company and initiative supporter. (Courtesy of Greene County African-American Museum Archives.)

In 1999, Daryl Barksdale and Michael Miller (Georgia Historic Preservation Division) present a check to the Dr. Calvin M. Baber Restoration Initiative. The following are pictured from left to right: Ruby Jackson, Vanessa Jones, Lucille Hudson, Lucille Tyson, Mary Breeding, Jackie Richardson, and Mamie Hillman. This Heritage 2000 Grant was used to begin the restoration project. (Courtesy of Greene County African-American Museum Archives.)

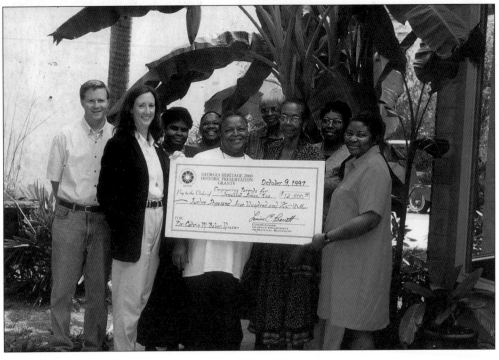

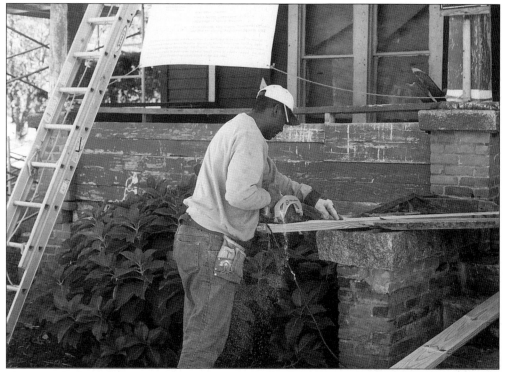

Above, Whitfield Brown, contractor, begins restoration of the dilapidated roof of the Dr. Calvin M. Baber historical home. (Courtesy of the Greene County African-American Museum Archives.)

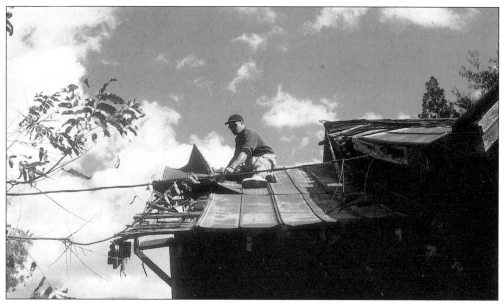

Contractor Stanford McMurray removes the dilapidated roof of Dr. Calvin M. Baber's home in this photo. The damage to the roof was more extensive than projected at the beginning of the project. (Courtesy of Greene County African-American Museum Archives.)

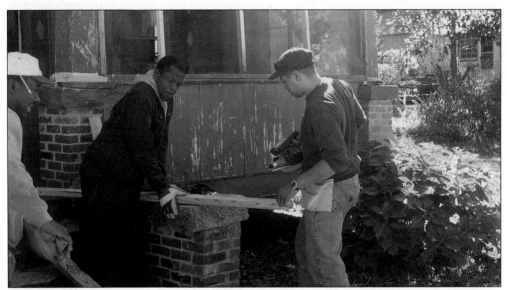

Contractors Whitfield Brown, Stanford McMurray, and an unidentified employee continue working on Dr. Baber's home. (Courtesy of the Greene County African-American Museum Archives.)

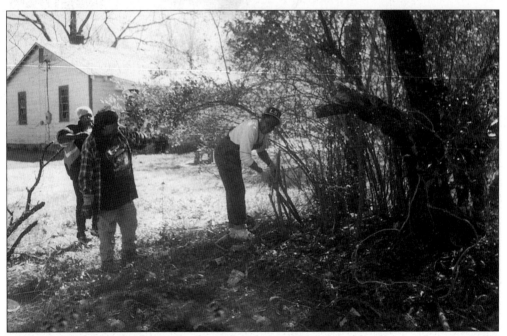

When restoration of the Dr. Calvin M. Baber home began, the yard was in a very littered and trashy condition. Through the years, the home had become a haven for drugs and alcohol. The restoration of Dr. Baber's home is the beginning of revitalization in the Railroad community of Greensboro. It has brought a sense of pride and concern about where and how residents view the community. In this photograph, Lucille Tyson and Odessa Franklin work tirelessly to clear the yard of debris. (Courtesy of the Greene County African-American Museum Archives.)

Mamie Hillman, Baber House Restoration Initiative director, installs a "No Trespassing" sign on the porch. (Courtesy of the Greene County African-American Museum Archives.)

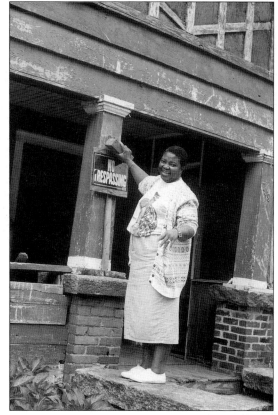

Dr. Calvin M. Baber's home begins to look much better. This historical structure is a tangible remnant of Greene County's African-American history. It is only one of two historical structures in the community that remains today and is listed on the National Register of Historical Places. (Courtesy of the Greene County African-American Museum Archives.)

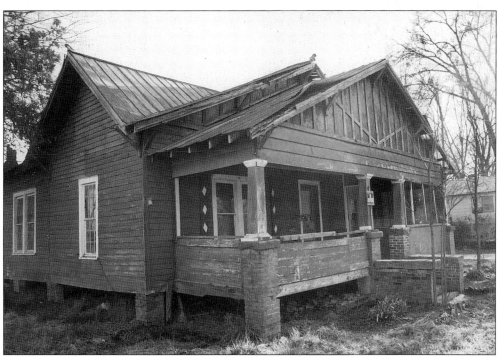

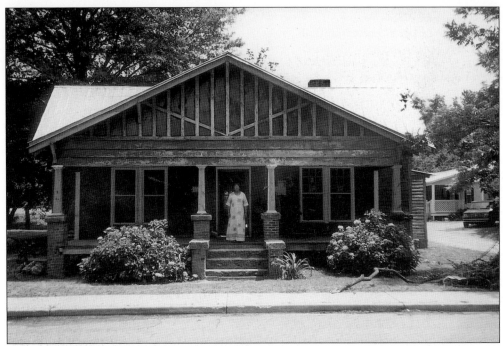

Mamie Hillman, Baber House Restoration Initiative director, is amazed at the progress of the restoration as she stands on the front porch. The vision is actively coming to fruition. (Courtesy of the Greene County African-American Museum Archives.)

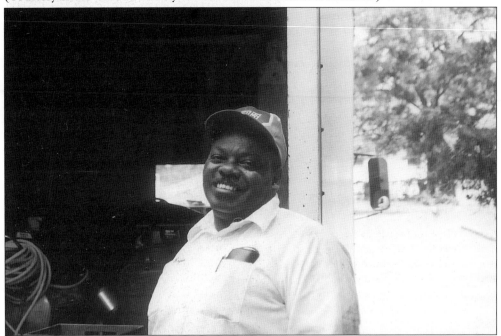

Roger Callaway, owner of Callaway Heating & Air Conditioning in Social Circle, Georgia, begins the first phase of the installation of central heating and air in the Dr. Baber historical home. (Courtesy of Greene County African-American Museum Archives.)

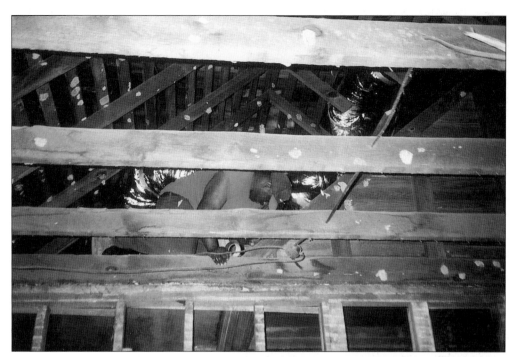

Roger Callaway's son is busy installing ducts in the interior of Dr. Baber's house. (Courtesy of Greene County African-American Museum Archives.)

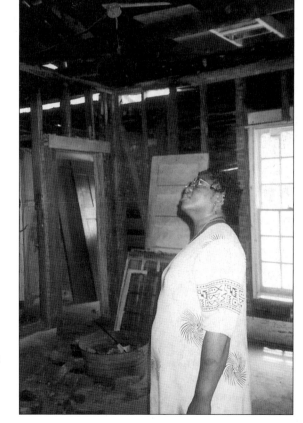

Project director Mamie Hillman views completed work at the Baber House. She always contemplates the next phase. The adaptive use of this building is a great achievement for Greene County. When completed this historical structure will house the Greene County African-American Cultural Museum and Resource Center, Inc. (Courtesy of Greene County Museum Archives.

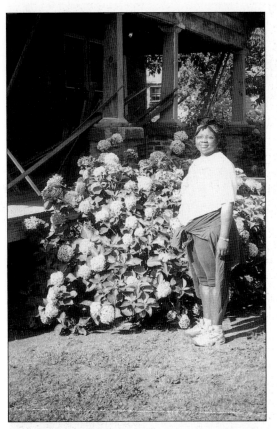

Mamie Hillman, project director, views the yard after mowing it. Each Saturday is a Baber House workday for her. She is truly committed to the task of making sure that this project is completed. (Courtesy of Greene County African-American Museum Archives.)

Contractor Ricky Robbins and his crew begin painting the exterior of the Dr. Calvin M. Baber historical home. (Courtesy of the Greene County African-American Museum Archives.)

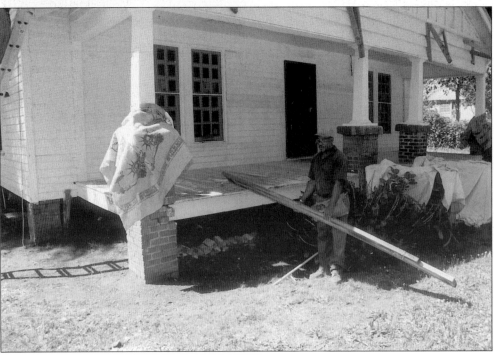

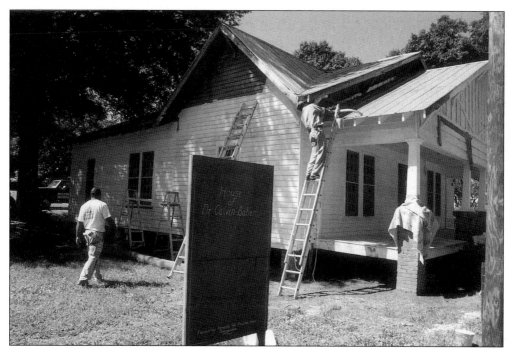

Contractor Ricky Robbins's crew continues painting the exterior of Dr. Baber's house. (Courtesy of Greene County African-American Museum Archives.)

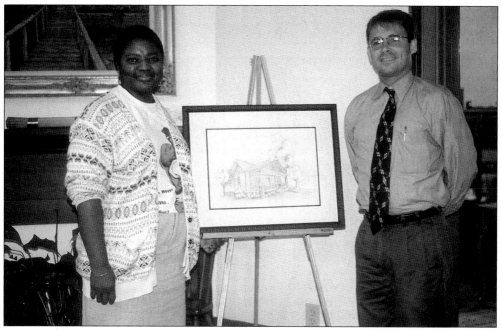

Mamie Hillman and Burk Walker (NRDC) stand beside a framed stretch of the Dr. Calvin M. Baber historical home depicting its completed restoration. Local architect and artist Sandra Hunt contributed her support and time to complete this beautiful stretch. (Courtesy of the Greene County African-American Museum Archives.)

Above is the marriage certificate of Dr. A.T. Chisolm and Claudia Byrd, dated July 4, 1912. (Courtesy of Greene County African-American Museum Archives.)

The death certificate of Dr. A.T. Chisolm is dated January 30, 1921. (Courtesy of Greene County African-American Museum Archives.)

The gravesite of Dr. A.T. Chisolm was discovered in the cemetery behind Springfield Baptist Church in the Canaan community. (Courtesy of Greene County African-American Museum Archives.)

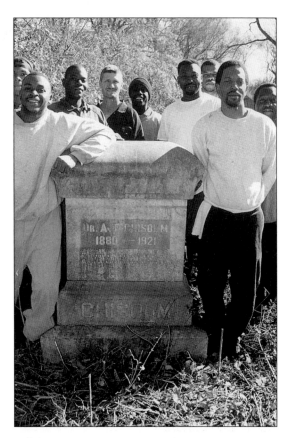

Mamie Hillman and an officer with the Greene County Sheriff's Department stand beside Dr. Chisolm's headstone. After the grave was cleaned off, Watts Funeral Home donated a granite marker, which is inscribed "Greene County's First African-American Physician." This marker was installed in front of the original tombstone. (Courtesy of Greene County African-American Museum Archives.)

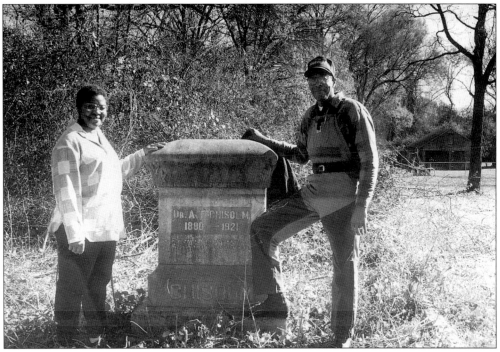

PRELIMINARY EDUCATION BLANK

Meharry Medical College:

This is to Certify, that _Calvin Melvin Baber_
(Full Name)

of No._____ Street, _Milstead Alabama_ is a person of good moral character,
(Town or City and State)

that ____he was in regular attendance at _Walden University_
(Name of High School, Academy or College)

located in _Nashville Tenn._ during the years _1916 — 1917_
(City and State) (Kindly specify school sessions, e. g., 1901-2, 1902-3, 1903-4, etc.)

that ____he satisfactorily completed the following specified courses, and that ____he was graduated from this institution in 19____

I hereby certify that the following is a correct and true statement of the record of the above named person, and worthy of full credence, as I verily believe.

Dated at _Nashville Tenn._ Signed _C F Garrett_
(Town or City and State)

Date _October 1_ 1917 Official Position _Registrar_

BRANCHES OF STUDY	TEXT-BOOK USED	AMOUNT COVERED (Please state definitely)	*In What Year Taken	No. of Weeks Pursued	No. of Periods a Week	Length of Periods in Minutes	Grade Given
English Grammar..........							
Composition and Rhetoric...							
History of English Literature							
English Classics...........							
Latin Grammar and Reader							
Cæsar...............Books							
Cicero..............Books							
Virgil..............Books							
Composition...........Pages							
German Grammar and Reader	Bacon	Text 1	1917	32	5	60	75
Second Year German........							
Third Year German.........							
Fourth Year German........							
Other Language, First Year							
Second Year................							
Third Year.................							
Fourth Year................							

7-14-16—1,000 * Kindly specify school session, e. g., 1901-2, 1902-3, etc.

This is the transcript of Dr. Calvin Melvin Baber at Meharry Medical School from 1911 to 1912. (Courtesy of Greene County African-American Museum Archives.)

Branches of Study	Text-Book Used	Amount Covered (Please state definitely)	*In What Year Taken	No. of Weeks Pursued	No. of Periods a Week	Length of Periods in Minutes	Grade Given
Mathematics, Algebra (Through Quadratics)							
Algebra, through logarithms							
Geometry, plane							
Geometry, solid							
Plane Trigonometry	Wentworth's	Text	1917	16	5	60	83
Conic Sections							
History, United States, Civics							
General History							
Ancient History							
Medieval and Modern							
History of England							
History of France							
....							
Science: Physics College	Wentworth & Hill	Text	1917	32	5	60	91
Laboratory Note Book							
Chemistry College	Hessler & Smith	"	1917	32	5	60	82
Laboratory Note Book							
Zoology							
Botany							
Biology College	Smallwood	Text	1917	32	5	60	91
Physiology							
Geology							
Astronomy							
Economics							
Psychology							
Ethics							
Logic							
Bible							
Other Subjects							

* Kindly specify school session. e. g., 1901-2, 1902-3, etc.

This is the transcript of Dr. Calvin Melvin Baber at Meharry Medical School from 1913 to 1914. (Courtesy of Greene County African-American Museum Archives.)

Branches of Study	Text-Book Used	Amount Covered (Please state definitely)	*In What Year Taken	No. of Weeks Pursued	No. of Periods a Week	Length of Periods in Minutes	Grade Given
Mathematics, Algebra (Through Quadratics)			1912-13	34	4	45	
Algebra, through logarithms..			1915-16	17	4	55	80
Geometry, plane............	Wentworth-Smith	Comp	1914-15	34	5	45	91
Geometry, solid............	do.	"	1915-16	17	3	55	74
Plane Trigonometry.........							
Conic Sections.............							
History, United States, Civics	Below						
General History............							
Ancient History...........	Botsford	Compl.	1912-13	34	5-4	45	88
Medieval and Modern.......	Myers	"	1914-15	34	5	45	73
History of England........							
History of France.........							
....							
Science: Physics...........	Milliken & Gale	Comp.	1915-16	34	5	45	72
Laboratory Note Book......							
Chemistry	Johnston	Comp	1914-15	34	5	55	85
Laboratory Note Book.......							
Zoology							
Botany	Hunter	Camp	1914-15	17	4	55	83
Biology	Hunter		1911-12	34	5	45	73
Physiology	Human Body	"	1915-16	17	4	55	82
Geology							
Astronomy							
Economics							
Psychology							
Ethics							
Logic			1911-1912 Each				
Bible I, II, III.........			1915	17	2	45	77
Other Subjects...........							
Civics	James & Sanford	Comp	1914-15	17	4	45	82
Economics	Burch & Nearing	"	1915-16	17	5	45	73

* Kindly specify school session, e. g., 1901-2, 1902-3, etc.

This is the transcript of Dr. Calvin Melvin Baber at Meharry Medical School in 1915. (Courtesy of Greene County African-American Museum Archives.)

Questions answered, where record is kept.

PRELIMINARY EDUCATION BLANK

Meharry Medical College:

This is to Certify, That... *Calvin Melvin Baber*
(Full Name)

of No.......................... Street, *Milstead, Alabama* .... is a person of good moral character,
(Town or City and State)

that ...... he was in regular attendance at *Talladega College, Preparatory Department*
(Name of High School, Academy or College)

located in ...... *Talladega, Alabama* ...... during the years *1911-12, 1912-13, 1914-15, 1915-16*
(City and State)   (Kindly specify school sessions, e. g., 1901-2, 1902-3, 1903-4, etc.)

that ...... he satisfactorily completed the following specified courses, and that ...... he was graduated from this institution in 19*16*.

I hereby certify That the following is a correct and true statement of the record of the above named person, and worthy of full credence, as I verily believe.

Dated at... *Talladega, Ala.,* ...... Signed......... *O. C. Silsby*
(Town or City and State)

Date *August 9*......, 1916. ...... Official Position *Secretary of Faculty*

BRANCHES OF STUDY	TEXT-BOOK USED	AMOUNT COVERED (Please state definitely)	*In What Year Taken	No. of Weeks Pursued	No. of Periods a Week	Length of Periods in Minutes	Grade Given
English Grammar............			1914-15	17	5	45	82
Composition and Rhetoric....	*Shackford-Judson*		1911-12	34	5	45	83
History of English Literature	*Long*		1914-16	51	4	45	77
English Classics..............							
Amer - Literature	*Hallick*		1912-13	34	4	45	80
Eng - Narration + Descrip"	*Baker*		1915-16	34	3	55	74
Latin Grammar and Reader..	*Bennet*		1911-12	34	5	45	78
Caesar ....Books	*Fowle -*		1912-13	34	5	45	76
Cicero ....Books	*Johnston*		1914-15	34	5	45	75
Virgil ....Books	*Greenough*		1915-16	34	5	45	78
Composition ....Pages							
German Grammar and Reader							
Second Year German........							
Third Year German.........							
Fourth Year German........							
Other Language, First Year..							
Second Year................							
Third Year.................							
Fourth Year................							

This is the transcript of Dr. Calvin Melvin Baber at Meharry Medical School in 1916. (Courtesy of Greene County African-American Museum Archives.)

Dr. Calvin Melvin's death certificate is dated November 22, 1945. (Courtesy of Greene County African-American Museum Archives.)

The obituary of Dr. George Calvin Lawrence is shown here. (Courtesy of Lucille Jones.)

Obituary

Dr. George C. Lawrence was a native of Greensboro, Georgia, the youngest son of Mr. and Mrs. Noel Lawrence. He was a graduate of Morehouse College, Meharry Medical School, and completed his internship at Homer G. Phillips Hospital. As a young adult, George joined Ebenezer Baptist Church and was an active member for over fifty years.

George began his professional career with the New York Department of Education. He later established his practice in Obstetrics and Gynecology in Greene County, Georgia. His work included service as Chief of Obstetrics and Gynecology at Southside Comprehensive Health Center in Atlanta. He also taught classes at Emory University School of Medicine. His staff memberships, prior to his retirement in 1996, included Crawford W. Long Hospital, Hughes Spalding Medical Center, Southwest Community Hospital, Parkway Regional Medical Center and Grady Memorial Hospital, all located in Atlanta, Georgia.

George served his Country with distinction as a Naval Officer and physician in the United States Navy Medical Corps where he held the rank of Lieutenant Commander.

He was an active member of several professional organizations. Those organizations included the American Medical Association, Georgia Medical Association, National Medical Association, Southern Medical Association, Obstetrics and Gynecological Society of Georgia and the Atlanta Medical Association, Inc. which presented him with the 1994 Service Award for fifty years of outstanding leadership, professionalism and dedication.

George also held memberships with many civic and social organizations including the Omega Psi Phi Fraternity, Inc., National Guardsmen, Inc., Pineacres Town and Country Club and The Hunter's Club.

George departed this life on Wednesday, January 6, 1999 and will be missed by those who survive him: his devoted wife, Helenda Ann Lawrence; daughters, Brenda Lawrence Harris (husband Robert) and Montrois Lawrence Parker (husband Stewart); son, Dr. George Lawrence, Jr.; stepson, Marion J. Jones (wife Angela); grandchildren, Robert Harris IV, Kimberly Harris, Angela Parker, Frankie Parker, Stephen Jones and Lauren Jones; great-granddaughter, Kymsasha Harris; niece, Gloria Knowles Bell; nephews, James A. Knowles and Lawrence E. Knowles; and a host of other relatives and friends.

Dr. C. M. Baber Dies Suddenly

Dr. C. M. Baber, well known Greensboro Negro physician, died suddenly in Atlanta Thursday afternoon.

Dr. Baber was witnessing a football game between two negro college elevens. Becoming ill, he was taken to an auto and died before reaching the hospital.

Dr. Baber located in Greensboro in 1921, coming here after the death of Dr. A. T. Chisolm, respected colored physician.

Here is the Greene County *Herald-Journal* newspaper article on Dr. Baber's death, printed on November 25, 1945. (Courtesy of *Herald-Journal* Archives, Greene County, Georgia.)

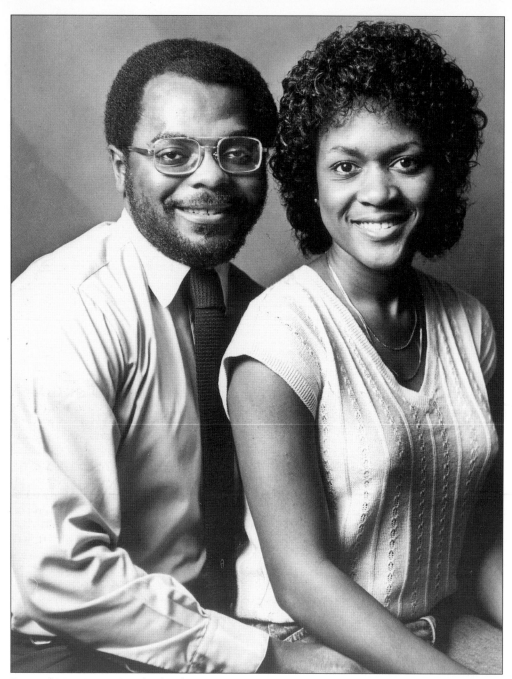

Dr. and Mrs. James Southerland are pictured above. Dr. Southerland is a native of McRay, Georgia, and his wife is a native of Rome, Georgia. Dr. Southerland is Greene County's fourth African-American physician. James and Debra have three lovely children. His practice is located below Minnie G. Boswell on Highway 15 South in Greensboro, Georgia. (Greene County African-American Museum Archives.)

Seven
COMMUNITY

It is so very hard to forget people who have been encouraging to you as a child. The old African proverb states, "it takes a village to raise a child." This remains true today. The home, school, and community play an important role in the lives of children. These could be considered the incubators for our children, for it is in these that children are reared to become productive citizens. We are all connected together throughout our lives, just as in the village where rain falls on all the huts, not just a few. Therefore, the end product of the lives of our children, whether the children become productive or not, affects all community members. Communities need to take ownership for their children as in former days. Children need to experience this because it encourages and nurtures the growth process in all of us.

People throughout the community have served many purposes in the lives of children. They are the informers who told parents when children misbehaved, and they provide wonderful memories when children become adults. Children become truly whole people when they experience this way of growing up. Each of us must remember that we are not an island unto ourselves. We are of one community, and it is our responsibility to be a part of the village that rears our sons and daughters. We are an extended family.

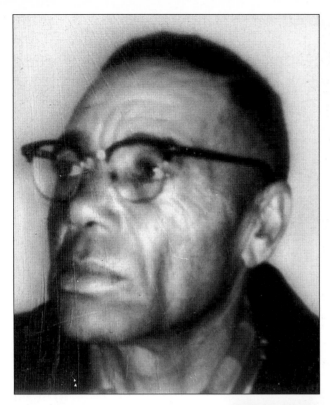

Joseph Armstrong was a public school bus driver for many years. He lived in the Veazey community. He operated his school bus safely and compelled all students who rode his bus to have good behavior. Armstrong was well respected and showed kindness to all. (Courtesy of Elgin Armstrong.)

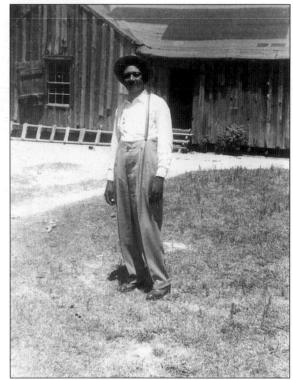

Uncle Charlie Ed Swain lived in the White Plains community. He always walked with his hands behind his back; he could be recognized from a far distance because of this. (Courtesy of Mrs. Edna Kilpatric.)

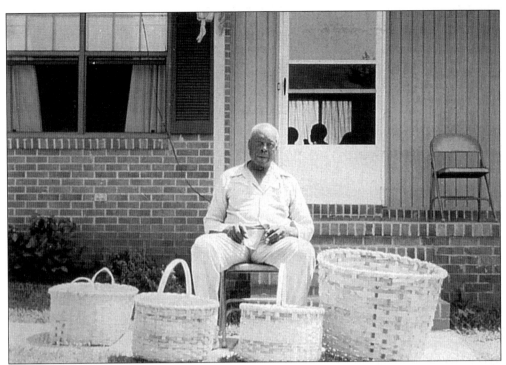

Waymon Miller, a lifelong resident of Greene County, was an excellent basket maker. His lovely wife is Hattie Miller. Many Green Countians and others are proud owners of his handmade baskets. (Courtesy of Greene County Chamber of Commerce.)

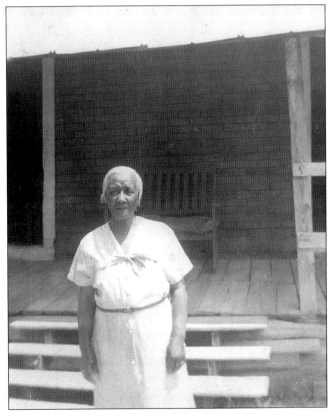

Aunt Fleta Ashley, a beloved lady, loved flowers, and even in her later years, she would sit in a chair in her flowerbeds and pull weeds. She is the daughter of former slaves, Enos and Eva Lucky of the White Plains community. (Courtesy of Mamie Hillman.)

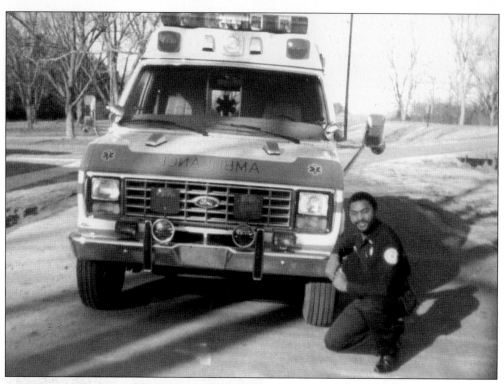

John L. Hillman Sr. was Greene County's first African-American emergency medical technician in 1984. He is a native of Warrenton, Georgia. (Courtesy of Mamie Hillman.)

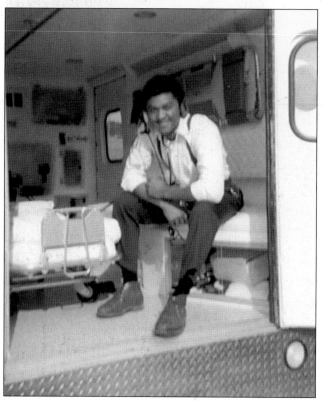

John L. Hillman Sr. is seated in the rear of Greene County's emergency medical technician vehicle. (Courtesy of Mamie Hillman.)

Elna Hutchinson, a Greene County native, became the first African-American clerk with the Greene County Board of Commissioners in 1999; she has been there ever since. (Courtesy of Elna Hutchinson.)

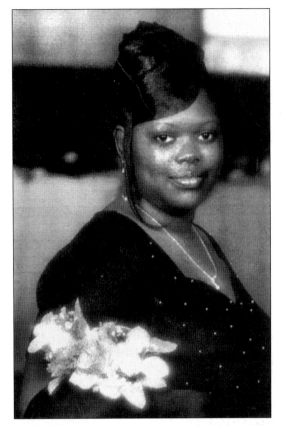

Greene County PRIDE (Parents Resource Institute of Drug Education) is a community-based group open to all high school students in Greene County. Members, like the students pictured below, make a personal commitment to remain alcohol and drug free as teenagers. (Courtesy of Cynthia Smith.)

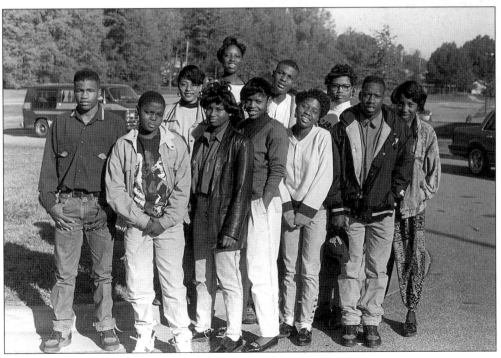

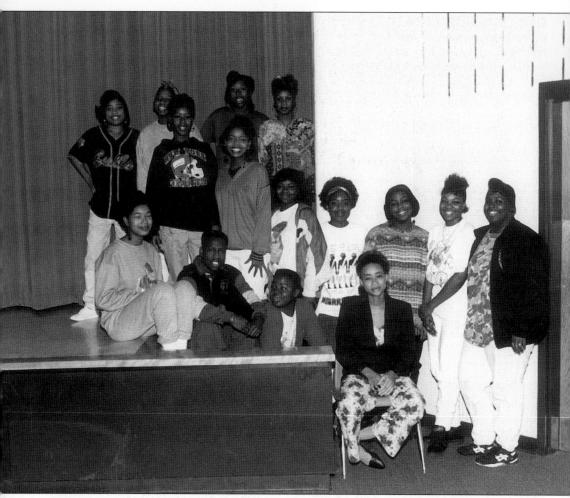

The Greene County PRIDE group poses for a picture in the high school Little Theater. The PRIDE Group meets each Monday evening from 6:00 p.m. until 8:00 p.m. They were blessed to travel to Drug Free Conferences in many states beyond Georgia. This is a wonderful group for the youth of Greene County. Cynthia Smith was director of the group; she had several parent volunteers through the years. (Courtesy of Cynthia Smith.)

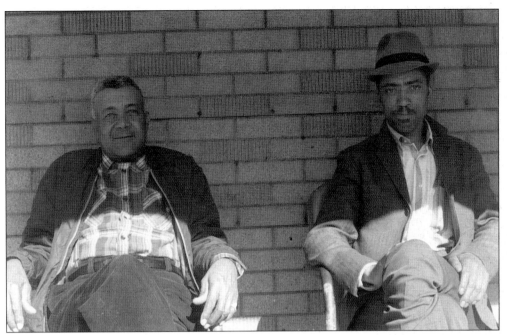

Charlie Ed Swain and George Zackery sit on a porch in White Plains, Georgia. George Zackery still resides in White Plains. (Courtesy of Mrs. Edna Kilpatric.)

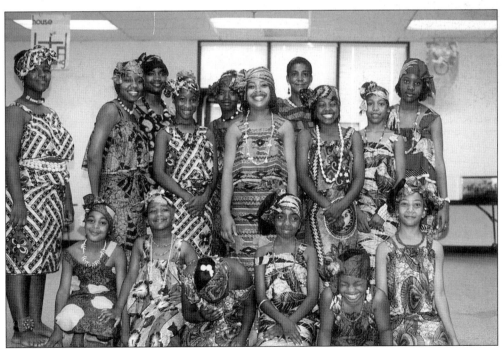

During the week of June 14, 1994, the Greene County PRIDE group sponsored an African Dance and Percussionist worship. Pictured here are some of the young girls who participated. For the performance, the PRIDE group purchased African fabric to make costumes. (Courtesy of Cynthia Smith.)

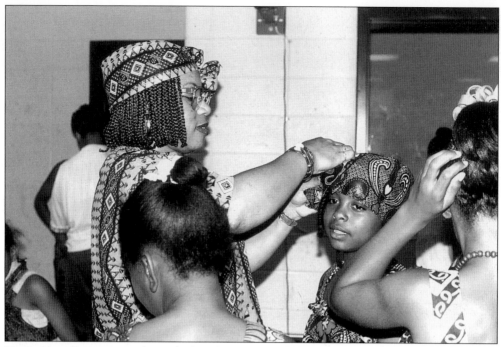

Mattie Terrell assists youths with their head wraps. Mattie lovingly made the dance outfits for the youth. (Courtesy of Cynthia Smith.)

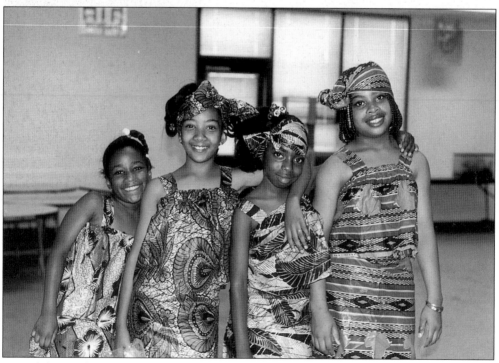

From left to right, Tarshe' Nesbitt, Brittany Rowland, Annie Ann Rhodes, and unidentified are dressed and ready to perform. They practiced all week for the occasion.

76

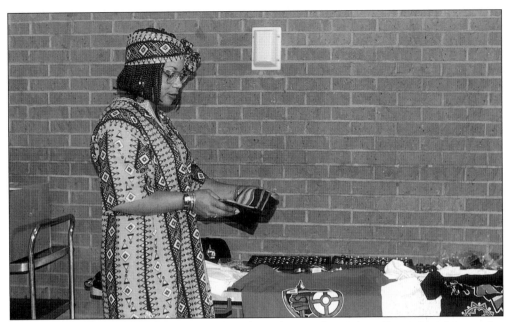

Mattie Terrell examines African crafts after the performance. Several artisans who create African jewelry, clothing, and other artifacts attended the program. (Courtesy of Cynthia Smith.)

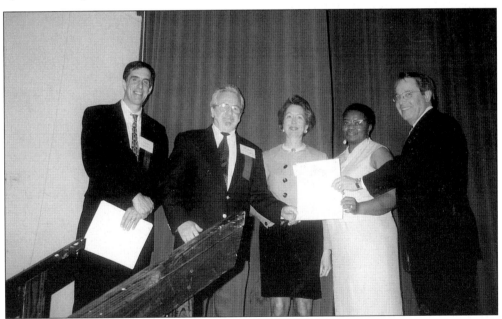

The City of Greensboro and the Dr. Calvin M. Baber Historical House Restoration Initiative is presented an award by the Georgia Trust for Historic Preservation on April 18, 1998. The following are pictured from left to right: Gregory Paxton, president and chief executive officer with the Georgia Trust; City of Greensboro mayor, Andrew Boswell; Mimi Vickers; Mamie Hillman; and Dexter Jordan, chairman of the Georgia Trust. (Courtesy of Georgia Trust for Historic Preservation.)

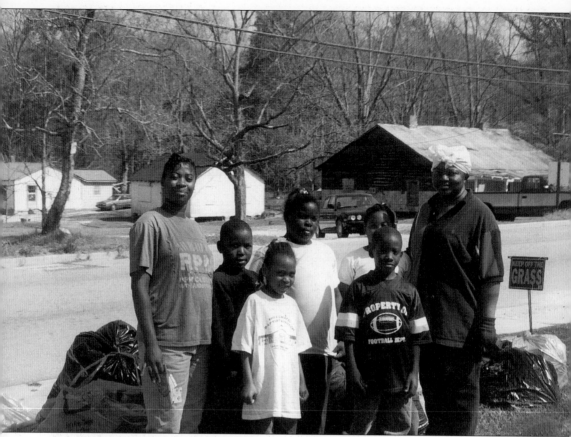

Since 1999, Mamie Hillman has sponsored a clean up campaign of the Railroad community in Greensboro. Each year the excited children actively participate in the campaign. The children pick up more bags of trash than any other groups throughout the community; therefore, they often win first prize in the campaign. The contributions are always donated to the Baber House Restoration Initiative. Pictured from left to right are Patricia Hall, Douglas Jones Jr., Kimberly Jones, Latonya Cochran, Raymond Cochran, Deandra Hurt, and Mamie Hillman. (Courtesy of Greene County African-American Museum Archives.)

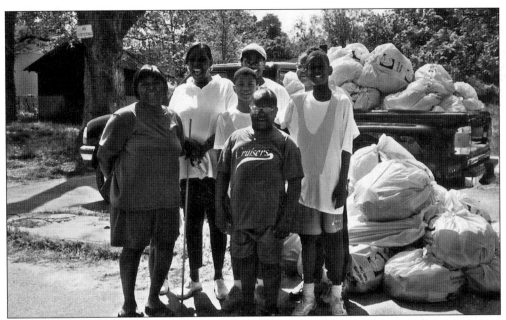

The Railroad Clean Up Campaign 2000 is busy working to clean up the neighborhood. Our neighborhoods are important because it is where we live and rear our families. Pictured from left to right are Karen Lewis, Gladys Carter, Jackie Richardson, Mamie Hillman, Latonya Cochran, Broderick Hurt, and Chris Griffin. (Courtesy of Greene County African-American Museum Archives.)

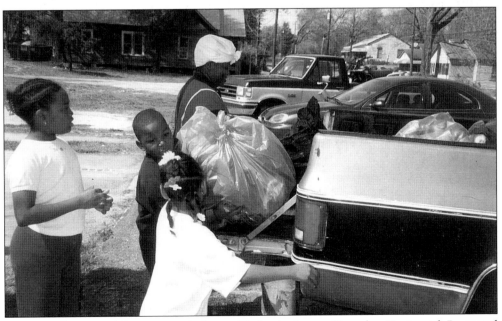

Mamie Hillman and her young helpers, Kimberly Jones, Deandra Hurt, and Raymond Cochran, load trash bags on the truck. These children volunteer every year. They are always excited about being part of the Clean Up Campaign. (Courtesy of Greene County African-American Museum Archives.)

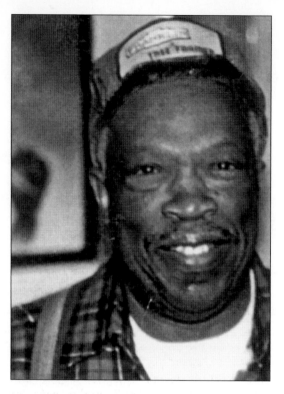

Charlie James Jones was a community member who provided transportation to people who did not have transportation of their own. His van service transported people near and far. There was no place that he would not transport anyone; he would take people to their physician, home, or just to the supermarket. Jones was a hard-working individual. He worked at Tom Gutherie Lumber Yard and drove a lumber truck for Jack Bradley. (Courtesy of Mrs. Lucille Tyson.)

On February 25, 1994, a memorial service was held at the Greene Taliaferro Comprehensive High School in memory of three young African-American students who lost their lives in September, October, and November 1993. Their deaths touched the hearts of the students and this community. These were wonderful young men who possessed all the keys to success. The Greene County Parent Support Group and the students sponsored the service. Mamie Hillman presented a plaque to the high school, inscribed with the following: "This plaque is presented to the Greene Taliaferro Comprehensive High School, students, friends and teachers in loving memory of Europe Manago, III, September 6, 1993; Dewayne Crawford Crawford, October 23, 1993; Aaron Glaze, Jr., November 27, 1993. Oh God, thank you that someday that the heartaches of this world will be left behind. Thanks too, for the reminder that because these young men believed in you; that they will one day join in your resurrection in their glorious new body and new life. AMEN." This photograph is of Aaron Glaze Jr., one of the young men who died during this period. (Courtesy of Greene County African-American Museum Archives.)

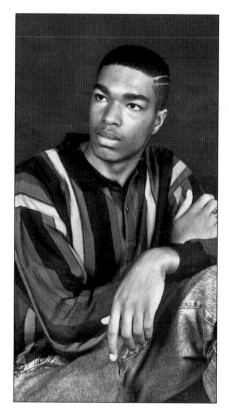

Eight
FAMILY

Family is the backbone of society. Families give birth to our churches, schools, and communities. Too often we neglect or forget the importance of family in our society or personal lives. We must begin to reconsider our priorities and change our thinking.

Family is about creating wonderful memories that will last for a lifetime, memories that become golden moments as our birthdays continue. Then we can reflect on those times shared with one another on special occasions or just "hanging out." Precious memories linger in our hearts. These are irreplaceable and are worth more than fine gold.

Families provide a map for individuals throughout their lifetime. They remind you of the wonderful attributes and training that parents placed in you, those little songs that you learned by heart, that grace you said before each meal, that prayer you said before going to bed at night, and the faces and character of all those family members. Even extended family was considered important. All of these persons shared a place and time in your life. We should never forget family; therefore, it is the responsibility of each of us to pass on our faith, love, truth, confidence, traditions, and memories to our sons, daughters, and their children.

We are all connected for we are accountable to our own families, as well as those in the community.

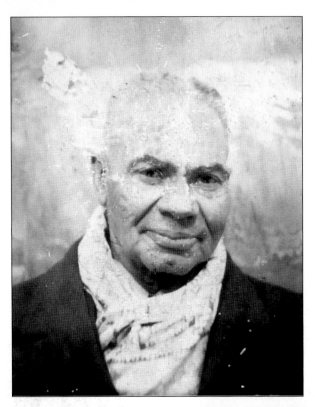

Henry Akars lived in the White Plains community but was born in Putnam County, Georgia. He and his mother and sister were brought to Greene County in wooden crates in the mid-1800s. (Courtesy of Mamie Hillman.)

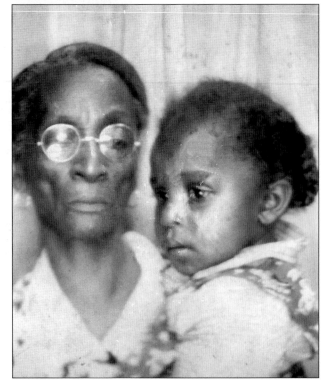

Amy (Thomas) Akars is a native of Hancock County, Georgia. Her parents relocated to Greene County in the late 1800s. Her granddaughter is pictured with her. (Courtesy of Mamie Hillman.)

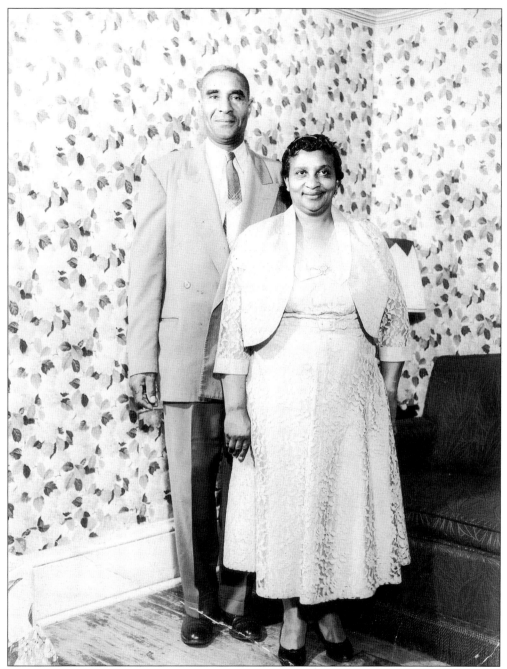

Joseph and Carrie (Akars) Ingram migrated to Evanston, Illinois, in the 1920s seeking better jobs. During this period, there was a mass migration of Southerners relocating to the northern states. Joseph was a native of Hancock County. (Courtesy of Lucille Johnson.)

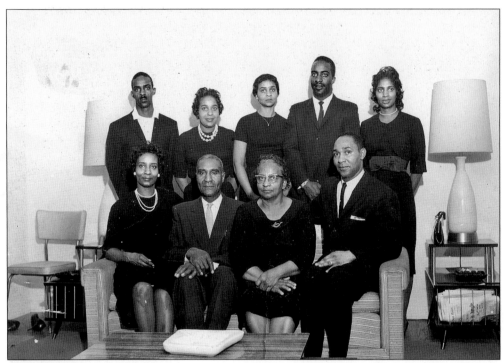

This Joseph and Carrie Ingram family photograph was taken in Evanston, Illinois. (Courtesy of Mamie Hillman.)

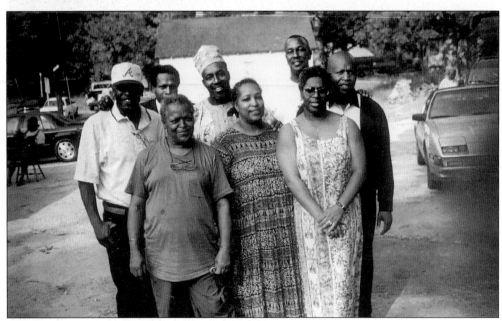

James and Wilma Jones Childers, from the Railroad community in Greensboro, Georgia, are pictured here with their family. From left to right are (front row) Lucille (Jones) Tyson, Bessie (Jones) Estrict, Jackie (Jones) Richardson, James Jones Jr., John Jones, Dave Jones, Emory Jones, and Luther Jones. (Courtesy Lucille Tyson.)

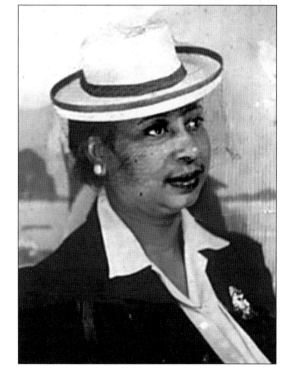

Above is the marriage certificate for Joseph Ingram and Carrie Akars; it is dated June 12, 1921. (Courtesy of Georgia Vital Records.)

Mattie (Akars) Swain migrated to Chicago, Illinois, in the 1920s seeking better opportunities for her family. (Courtesy of Mamie Hillman.)

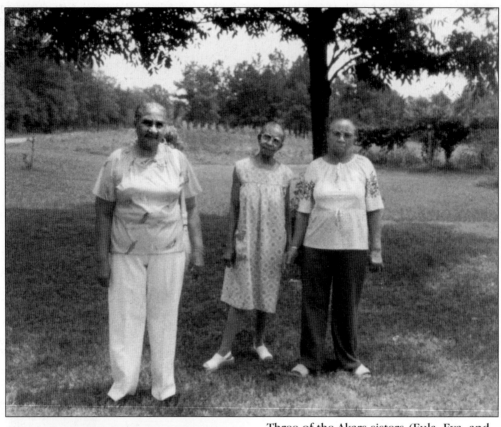

Three of the Akars sisters (Eula, Eva, and Ella) are pictured above. Eva Lucky migrated to Cincinnati, Ohio, during the 1920s for better job opportunities. Eula and Eva were visiting their youngest sister, Ella, at her home in White Plains, Georgia, when this photo was taken. (Courtesy of Mamie Hillman.)

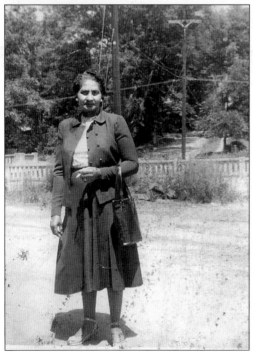

Eula (Akars) Thomas migrated to Chicago, Illinois, in the 1920s for more opportunities. (Courtesy of Lucille Davis.)

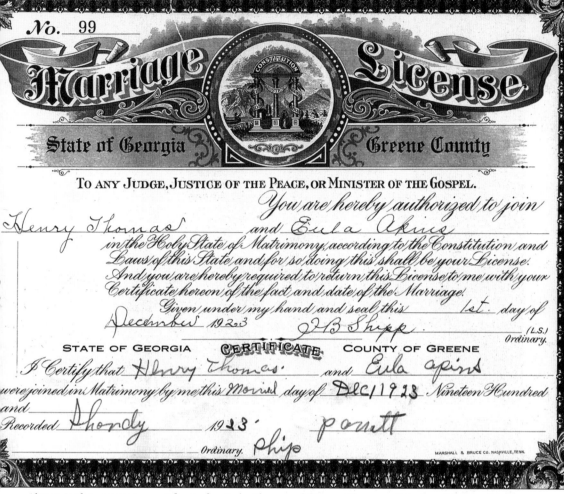

Above is the marriage certificate for Eula Akars and Henry Thomas; it is dated December 1, 1923. (Courtesy of Georgia Vital Records.)

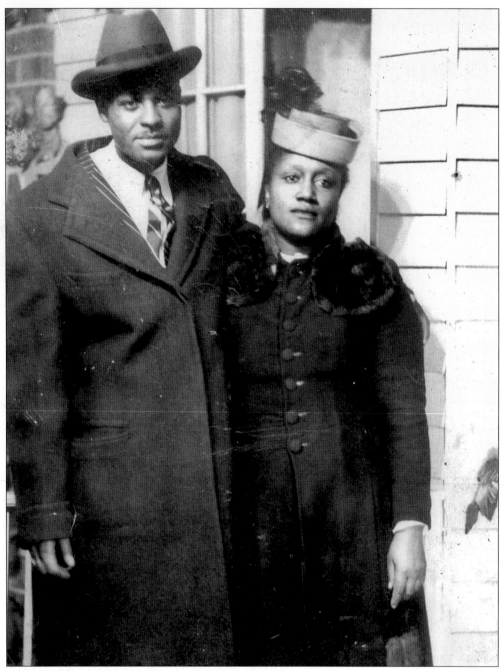

Alec and Willie Clara Champion lived in the White Plains community. Alec was killed in 1945 in Greene County. His body was found on the railroad tracks at Carey Station. His wife, Willie Clara, and their two sons relocated to New York in the Harlem area. (Courtesy of Hollis Champion.)

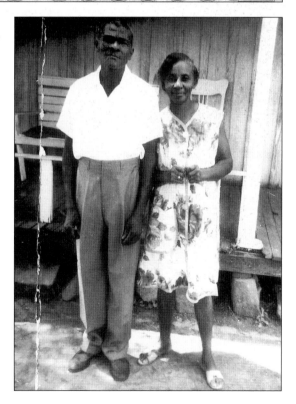

The marriage certificate for Alec Champion and Willie Clara Gordon is dated December 4, 1937. (Courtesy of Georgia Vital Records.)

Reid and Ella (Akars) Champion were lifelong residents of the White Plains community. They were parents of 11 children and worked very hard in the fields picking cotton and doing other jobs. Reid worked for Mell Jernigan's family for many years, did carpentry work with Levy Johnson of White Plains, mowed lawns throughout the community, and even traveled with his wife and others out of Greene County to pick cotton. Ella was a homemaker, worked in the fields, took in laundry, and did domestic work. (Courtesy of Wreath Neely.)

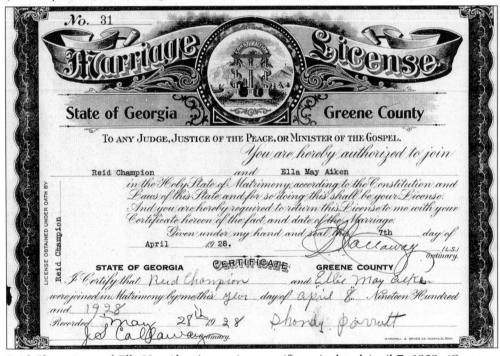

Reid Champion and Ella Mae Akars's marriage license application is dated March 31, 1928. (Courtesy of Mamie Hillman.)

Reid Champion and Ella Mae Akars's marriage certificate is dated April 7, 1928. (Courtesy of Mamie Hillman.)

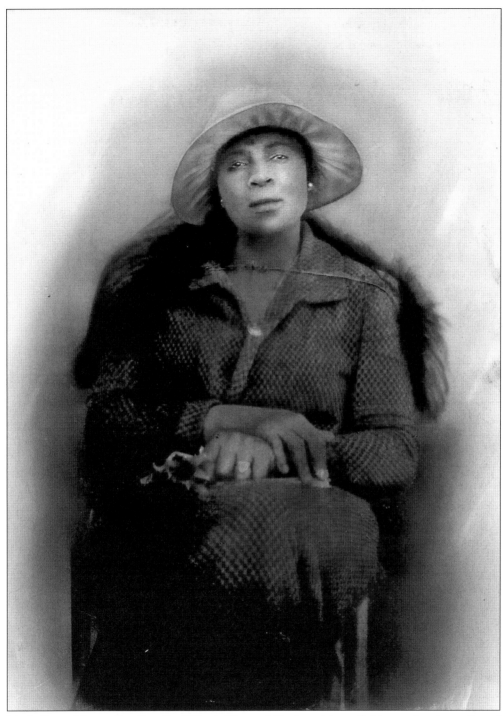

Lizzie Reynolds was fondly called "Lizzie Plump." She loved to go fishing on local ponds and creeks. (Courtesy of Lucille Johnson.)

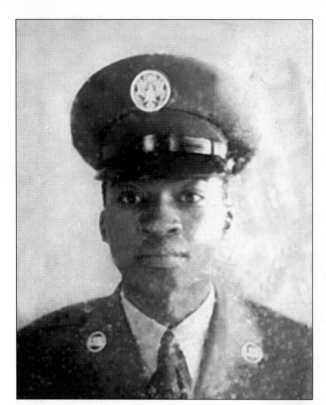

Revan Champion joined the United States Army after graduating from the local high school. After serving his country he relocated to New York. He returns often to visit family. (Courtesy of Mamie Hillman.)

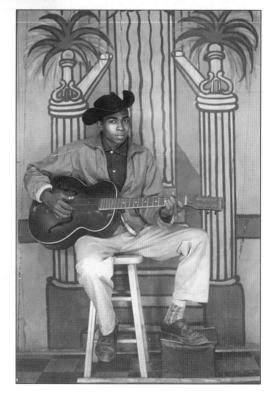

John Henry Champion, lovingly called "Bay," was named after both of his grandfathers (John Champion and Henry Akars). He loved to go fishing and hunting throughout the woodlands of Greene County. Bay also loved to play the guitar. (Courtesy of Mamie Hillman.)

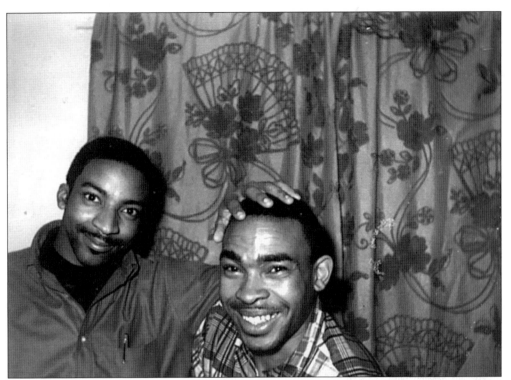

Armour and John Henry Champion share a laugh and a smile. (Courtesy of Marie Bryant.)

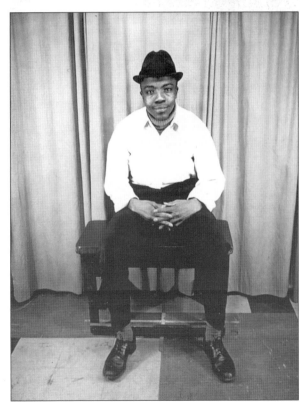

Willie Claude Champion relocated to Washington, D.C., by way of Atlanta, Georgia, after graduation. (Courtesy of Mamie Hillman.)

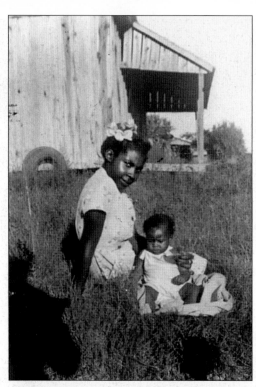

Marie Champion and her daughter pose in front of a wreath at their home in White Plains. (Courtesy of Mamie Hillman.)

Reid Champion tests the water before watering his potted plants. He was very good with flowers and any kind of plant. (Courtesy of Mamie Hillman.)

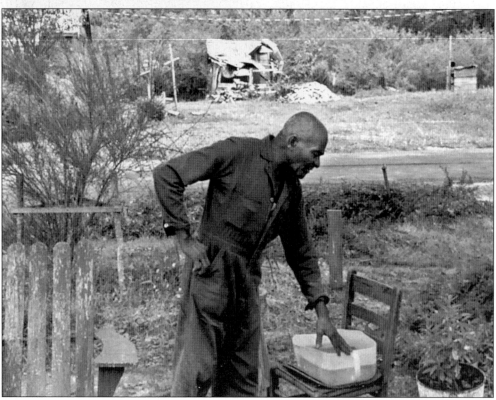

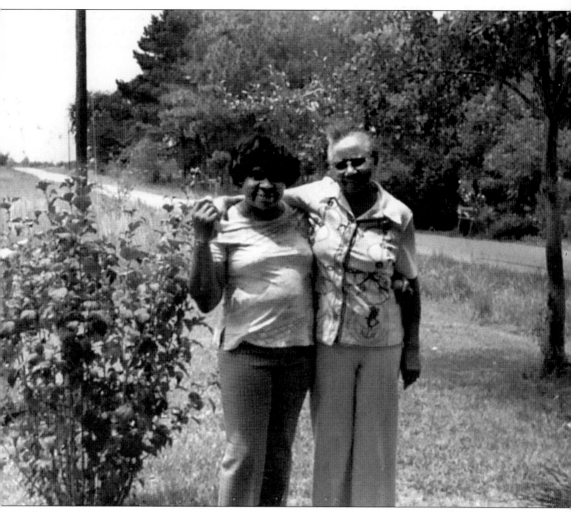

Ella Mae Champion and her eldest daughter, Marie Bryant, are pictured in their yard in White Plains, Georgia. (Courtesy of Mamie Hillman.)

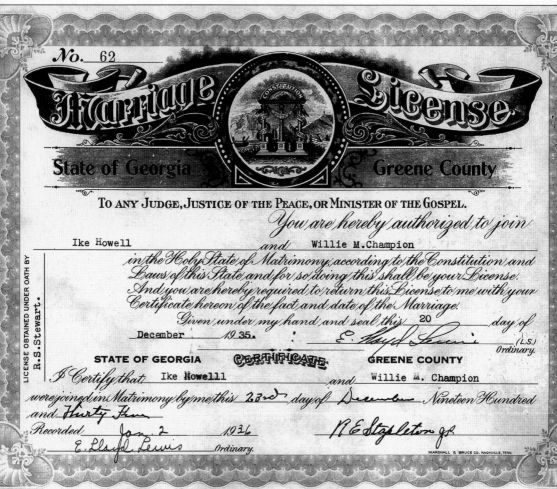

The marriage certificate of Ike Howell and Willie Mae Champion is dated December 20, 1935. Ike was a native of the Pittsburg community in White Plains; his mother was Josephine Jackson. The couple resided in the Harlem, New York, area. (Courtesy of Georgia Vital Records.)

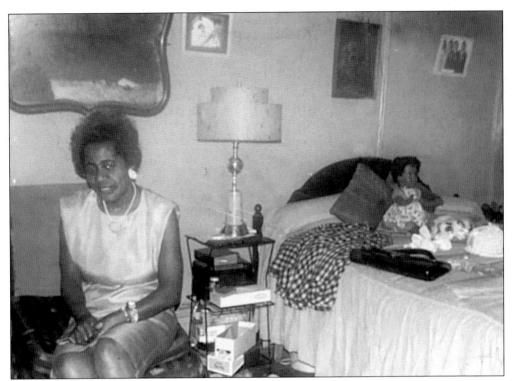

Willie Mae (Champion) Howell,
formerly from Greene County,
migrated to New York during the
1920s. (Courtesy of Mamie Hillman.)

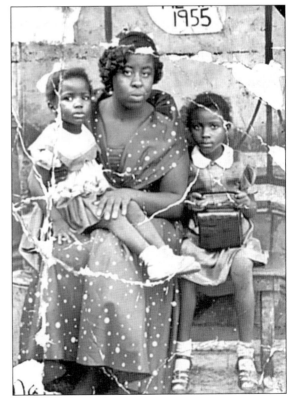

Mamie and Margaret Champion pose
with their cousin Mary Dean at the
Greene County Fair in 1955. The
county fair was an exciting time
when it came to any rural area.
(Courtesy of Mamie Hillman.)

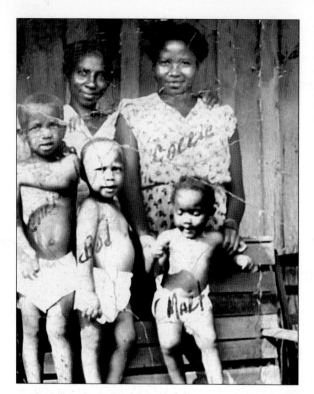

Ella Champion and daughters Carrie Bell and Margaret pose on the front porch of their house in White Plains, Georgia. The boys pictured are Earnest and Bud Davis (the children of Lucille Davis). (Courtesy of Mamie Hillman.)

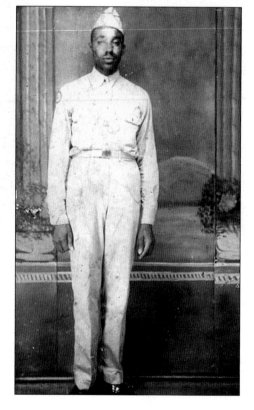

Clarence Dixon served in the United States Army for over 20 years. He was the son of Lizzie Reynolds of White Plains, Georgia. (Courtesy of Mamie Hillman.)

Amy Thomas and an unidentified friend are pictured here. Amy was the daughter of Lizzie Reynolds. She relocated to the New York area in the early 1930s. (Courtesy of Lucille Davis.)

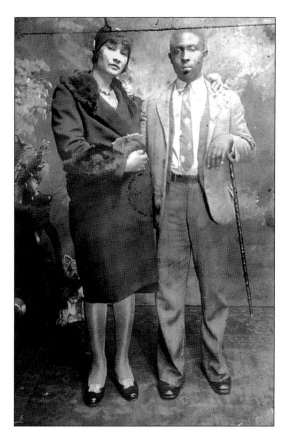

Evan "Zeke" Lawrence is pictured with his mule at his barn in the Greshamville community. (Courtesy of Wreath Neely.)

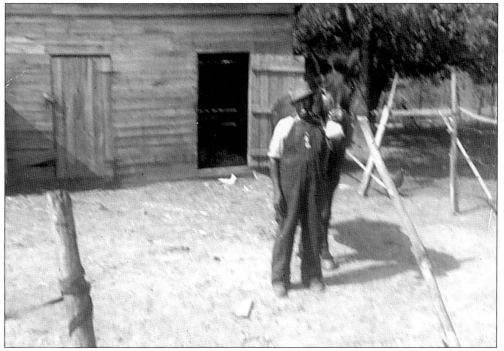

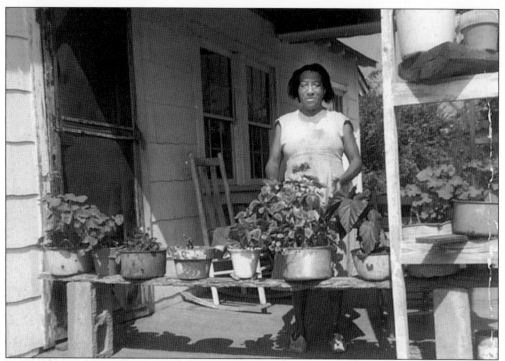

Lelia Lawrence admires her plants on her front porch in the Greshamville community. She loved beautiful flowers and was very good with them. (Courtesy of Wreath Neely.)

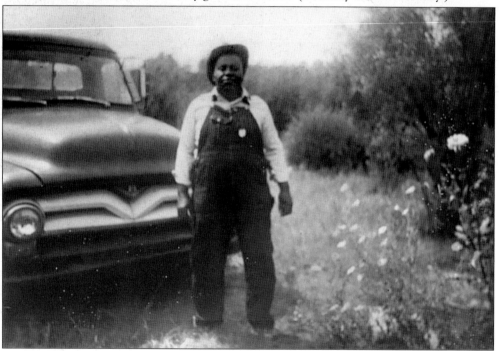

L.C. Raper ("Jack") is shown casing his truck in the Greshamville community. (Courtesy of Wreath Neely.)

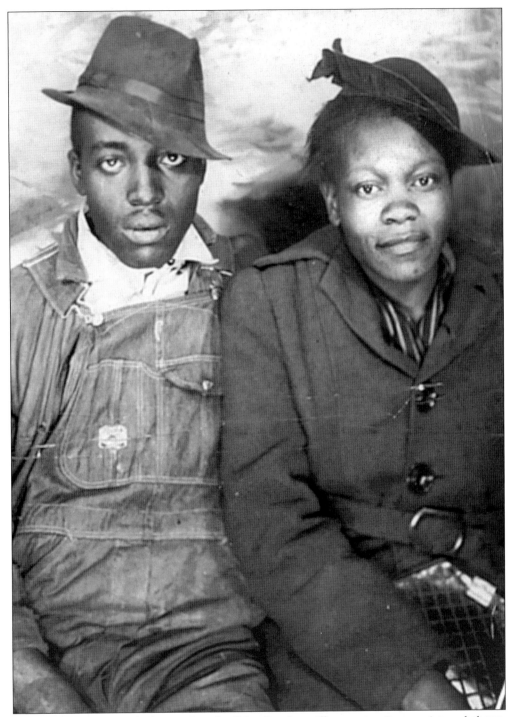

Le'mon Lawerence and Ida Mae Baugh of the Greshamville community are pictured above. Le'mon served in the United States Army until his death in the 1940s. He was the only son of Evan and Lelia Lawrence. (Courtesy of Wreath Neely.)

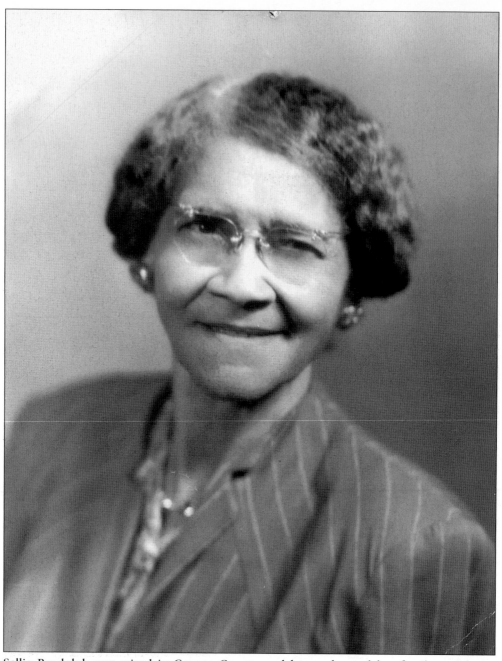

Sallie Randolph was raised in Greene County and later relocated her family to Atlanta. (Courtesy of Carrie Taylor.)

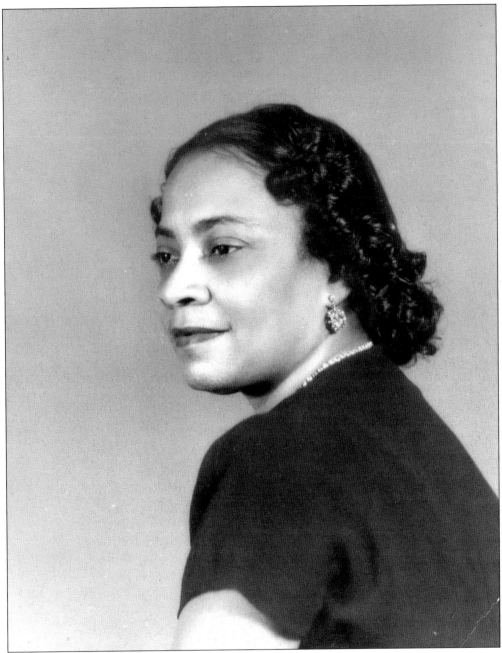

Sallie King, daughter of Sallie Randolph, is pictured in the 1930s. (Courtesy of Carrie Taylor.)

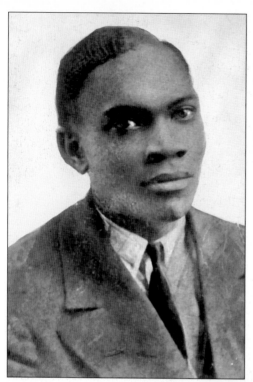

Willie Lee Lumpkin, son of Sallie Randolph, is pictured in the 1930s. (Courtesy of Carrie Taylor.)

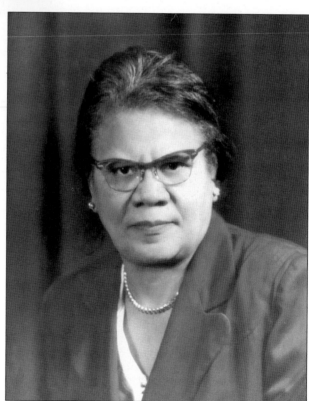

Orie Mapp, sister of Sallie Randolph, is pictured in the 1930s. She lived in Atlanta. (Courtesy of Carrie Taylor.)

The family of John and Mamie Hillman is pictured in the late 1980s. The Hillman children are Je'ohne, Lea, Julian, and John Jr. (Courtesy of Mamie Hillman.)

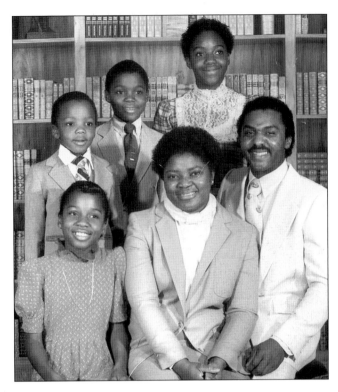

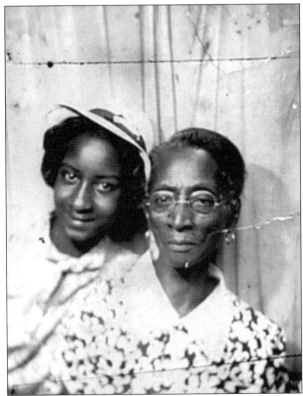

Amy Akars visits with one of her granddaughters. This photograph was taken in Evanston, Illinois, while Henry and Amy Akars were visiting their daughter Carrie Ingram, *c.* 1940s. (Courtesy of Mamie Hillman.)

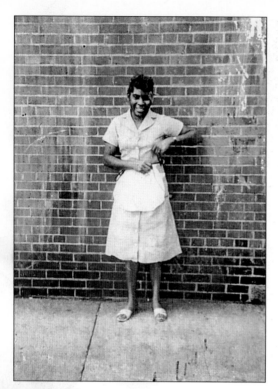

Marie Champion is photographed doing domestic work at a local hotel in downtown Cincinnati, Ohio, when she first arrived from Georgia. (Courtesy Marie Bryant.)

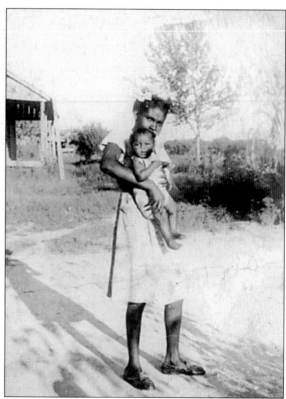

Marie Champion and her daughter, Wreath, are pictured at the Champions' home in White Plains, Georgia. (Courtesy of Marie Bryant.)

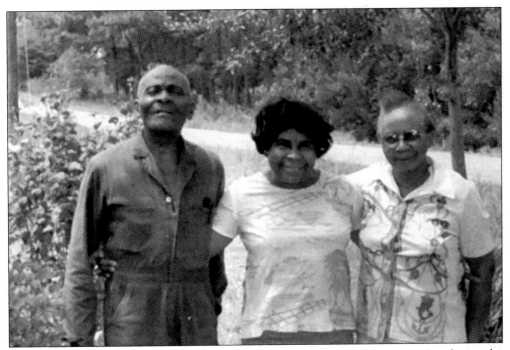

Reid and Ella Champion pose with their eldest daughter, Marie, who was visiting during the summer. (Courtesy of Mamie Hillman.)

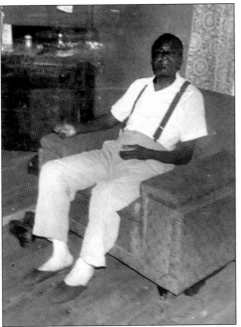

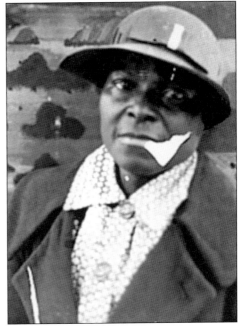

(above, left) John Champion of White Plains, Georgia, worked at the Minnie G. Boswell Hospital. After his wife died he relocated to the Canaan community in Greensboro. (Courtesy of Mamie Hillman.) *(above, right)* Mamie (Riddenberry) Champion of White Plains, Georgia, is pictured above. (Courtesy of Mamie Hillman.)

MARRIAGE LICENSE.

State of Georgia, County of Greene.

1902 - 16

To any Judge, Justice of the Peace, or Minister of the Gospel:

YOU ARE HEREBY AUTHORIZED TO JOIN

Johny Champion and *Mamie Rittenberry*

in the Holy State of Matrimony, according to the Constitution and laws of this State, and for so doing this shall be your license; and you are hereby required to return this license to me, with your certificate hereon of the fact and date of the marriage.

Given under my hand and seal, this *31st* day of *December*, 1901

Jas H Marhester (Seal.)
Ordinary.

STATE OF GEORGIA, GREENE COUNTY.   CERTIFICATE.

I certify that *Johny Champion* and *Mamie Rittenberry*

were joined in matrimony by me, this *1st* day of *January*, Nineteen Hundred and *Two*

H. W. Copeland Jr.

Recorded *Jun 21st*, 1902

Jas H Manhester, Ordinary.

Marriage Record B (Colored) Greene County.

The marriage certificate for John Champion and Mamie Riddenberry is dated December 31, 1901. They had four children. (Courtesy of Georgia Vital Records.)

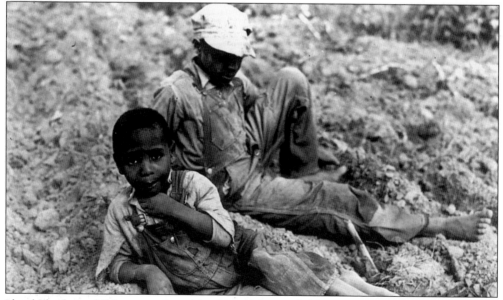

Lloyd Rhodes's children are pictured *c.* May 1941 in a field near their homes in the Bethany Church community. Lloyd Rhodes was a farmer in that area of Greene County. (Courtesy of Hargrett Rare Book and Manuscript Library, University of Georgia.)

John Larry Hillman Sr., former
Warrenton, Georgia native, is
pictured as an elementary school
student. John works with St. Mary's
Emergency Medical Service.
(Courtesy of Mamie Hillman.)

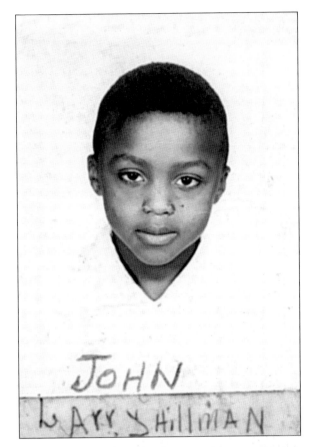

John and Mamie Hillman are
pictured at an ROTC banquet at
Greene Taliaferro Comprehensive
High School in 1994. Their son,
Julian, was a part of the first ROTC
class at the high school. (Courtesy
of Mamie Hillman.)

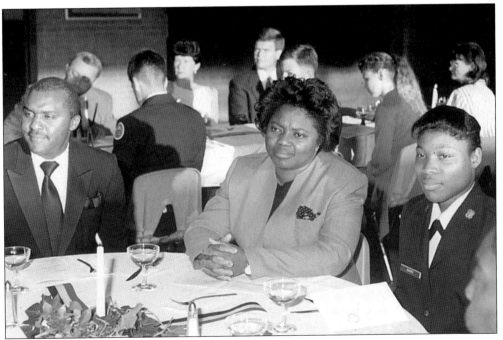

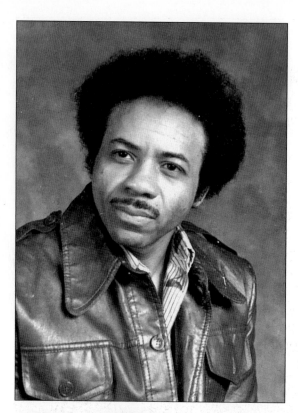

Willie Howell is the son of Eva Luckey of Cincinnati, Ohio. Willie was born in Greene County; however, his mother relocated to Ohio while he was still a child. (Courtesy of Mamie Hillman.)

Julian Hillman takes a break while off duty of the USS *Austin* in Norfolk, Virginia. He has been in the United States Navy for eight years and has re-enlisted for three more years. (Courtesy of Mamie Hillman.)

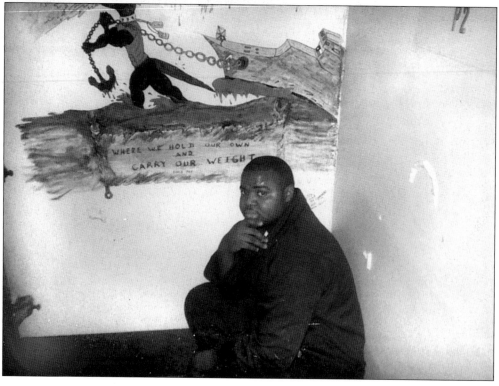

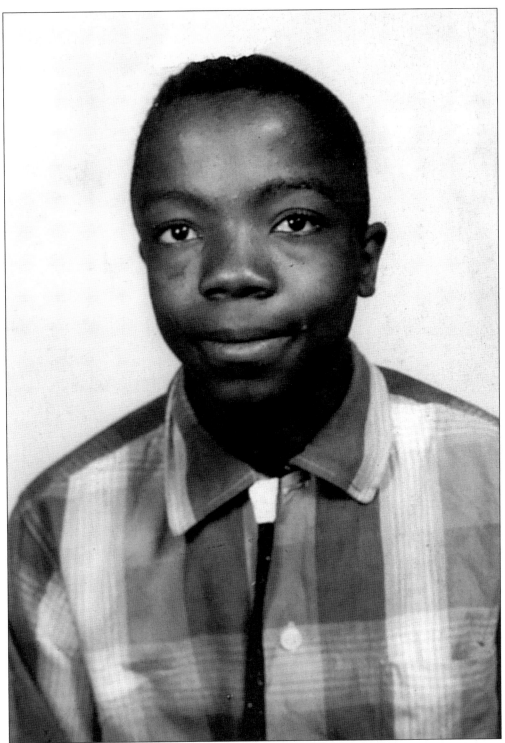

Willie C. Champion is pictured above as a high school student at F.T. Corry High School in Greensboro. (Courtesy of Mamie Hillman.)

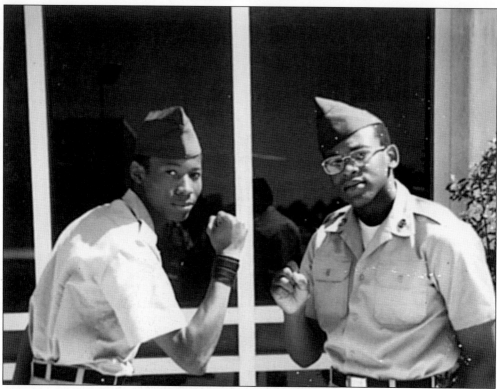

John Taylor is pictured with an unidentified friend in the U.S. Army. John is the eldest child of Joe B. and Carrie B. (Champion) Taylor of Atlanta. (Courtesy of Mamie Hillman.)

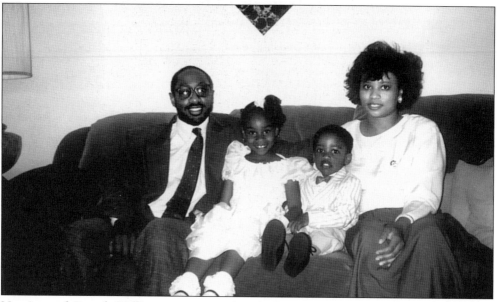

Maurice and Beverly Williams are pictured with their children Maurice Jr. and Nicole in Atlanta. Beverly is the daughter of Carrie B. (Champion) Taylor. (Courtesy of Mamie Hillman.)

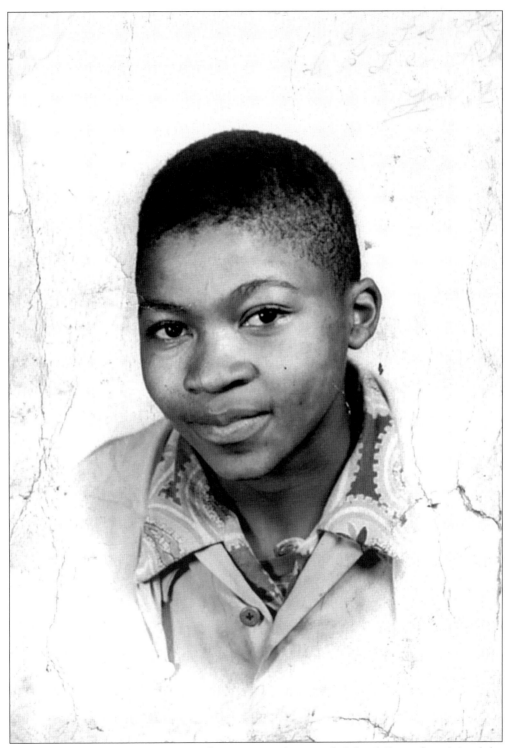

Revan Champion is pictured as a student at Greensboro High School. Revan later joined the U.S. Army. (Courtesy Mamie Hillman.)

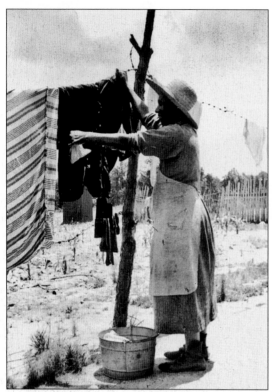

Dora Lawson was a native of Hancock County, Georgia. She and her husband Lee Lawson relocated to White Plains, Georgia, in the Pittsburg community. Dora was born on January 1, 1880; her parents were Redly Mosely and Emma Hall. Dora and her husband were the proud parents of nine daughters. Dora died on November 14, 1962; she was 82 years old. She is buried at the Mt. Zion Baptist Church in Hancock County, Georgia. She is pictured here c. May 1941. (Courtesy of Hargrett Library of Rare Books and Manuscripts, University of Georgia.)

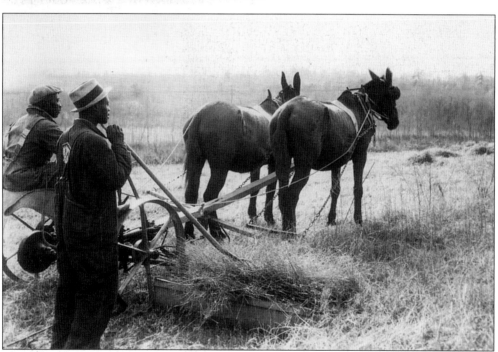

Dora Lawson's grandson is about to begin the fall plowing of their fields, c. September 1941. (Courtesy of Hargrett Library of Rare Books and Manuscripts, University of Georgia.)

John Hillman Sr. and John Hillman Jr.
are pictured at the Navy Pier in Norfolk,
Virginia. John's ship, the USS *Detroit*,
was docked there for a short time.
(Courtesy of Mamie Hillman.)

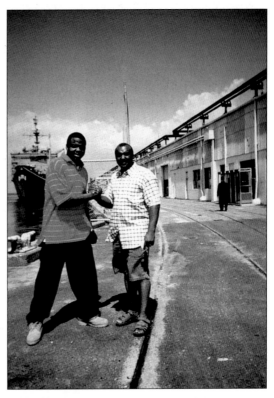

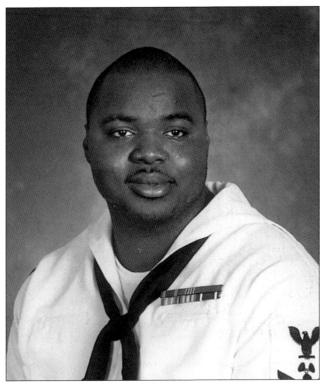

Julian Hillman, a member of
the United States Navy, is
pictured on the USS *Austin* in
Norfolk, Virginia. (Courtesy of
Mamie Hillman.)

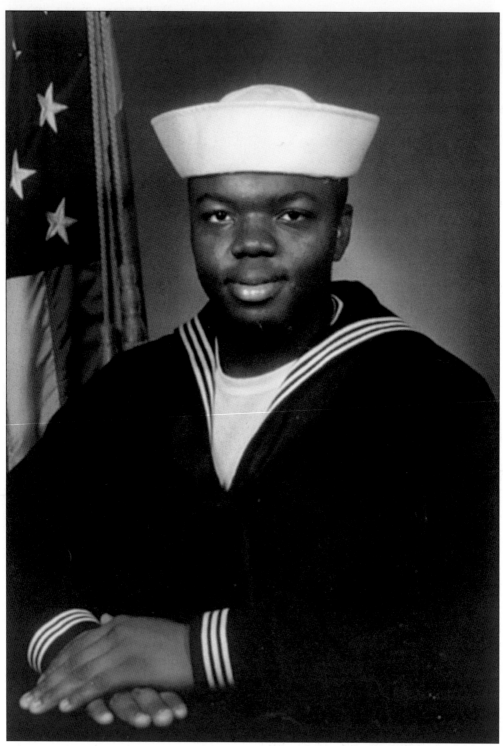

John L. Hillman Jr., a member of the United States Navy, is pictured on the USS *Detroit* in Earl, New Jersey. (Courtesy of Mamie Hillman.)

Pictured *c*. October 1935 are Lizzie and Enos Lucky, former slaves who lived in White Plains, Georgia. They were the parents of several children who later lived in the community. Their daughter Fleta Ashley is depicted in chapter seven. (Courtesy of Hargrett Library of Rare Books and Manuscripts, University of Georgia.)

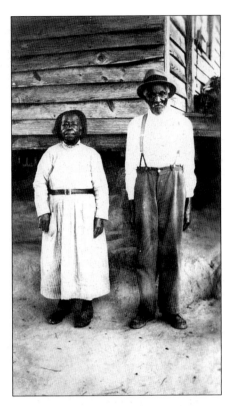

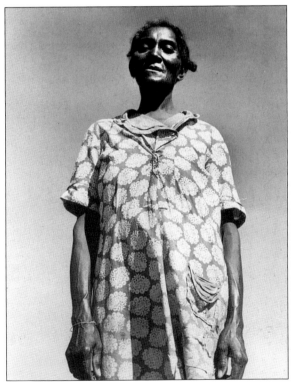

An unidentified tenant farm woman from the Woodville community of Green County stops for a photograph, *c*. June 1941. She was a widow and only had the assistance of her children in operating her farm. (Courtesy of Hargrett Library of Rare Books and Manuscripts, University of Georgia.)

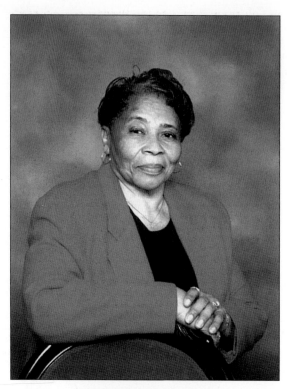

Carrie B. (Champion) Taylor is a Greene County native. (Courtesy of Carrie B. Taylor.)

Former slaves of Greene County stand in front of their home getting ready to use a plow in the late 1800s. They are husband and wife. (Courtesy of Arthur Raper Collection, Chapel Hill, North Carolina.)

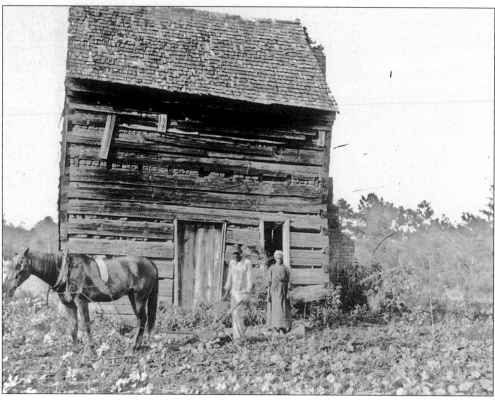

Mamie L. Hillman visits with her 8-month-old grandson, Daniel Lee Smith. He is the son of Lea and Bobby Smith Jr. of Columbia, South Carolina. (Courtesy of Lea Smith.)

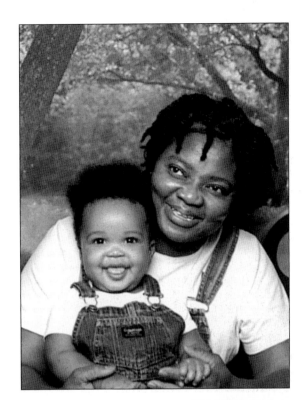

Oscar and Julia Hillman pose on the front porch of their home. (Courtesy of John Hillman Sr.)

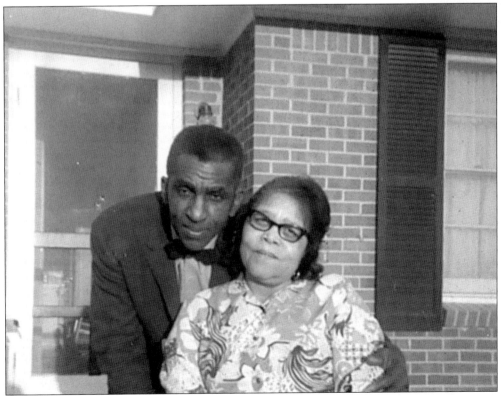

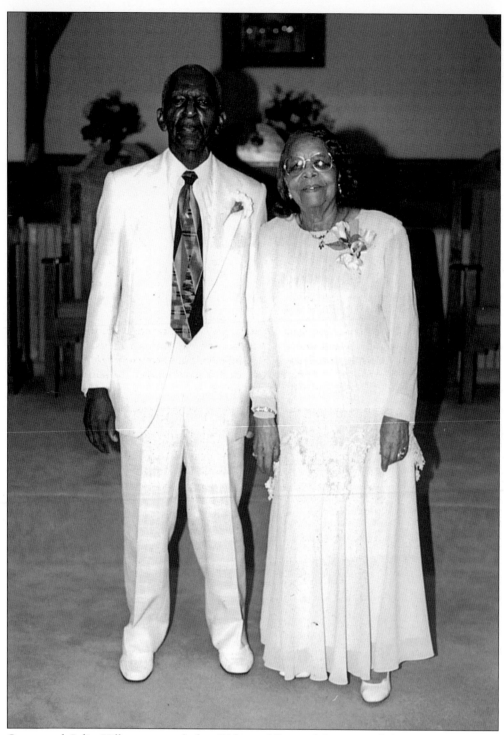

Oscar and Julia Hillman attend the 25th wedding celebration of their youngest son, John Hillman Sr., at Second Baptist Church in White Plains, Georgia. (Courtesy of Mamie Hillman.)

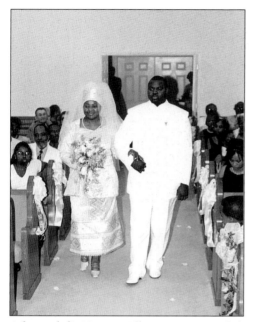

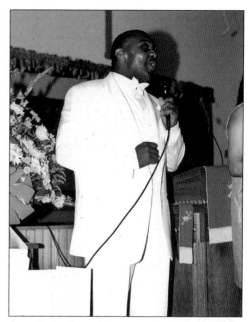

(above, left) Mamie Hillman is escorted down the isle by her eldest son for the wedding celebration. Her suit was made from African fabric. She had tiny cowrie shells sewn in the detachable train and headpiece. (Courtesy of Mamie Hillman.) *(above, right)* John Hillman Sr. sings "You Are So Beautiful" as Mamie is escorted down the aisle. The songs that he sang were a surprise to Mamie. (Courtesy of Mamie Hillman.)

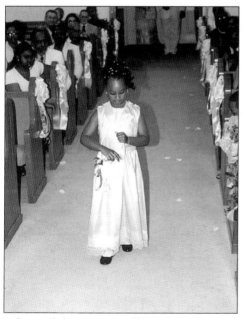

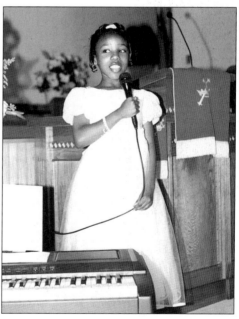

(above, left) Mamie Hillman's niece, Monica Sturkey's daughter, Ashley, made a lovely flower girl. (Courtesy of Mamie Hillman.) *(above, right)* Sierra King, the daughter of Ignatius King and Charlotte Wrice, sang beautifully. Tyrome Eaves was the musician for this occasion. (Courtesy of Mamie Hillman.)

121

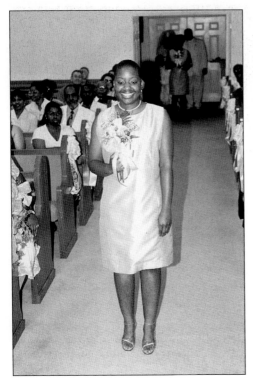 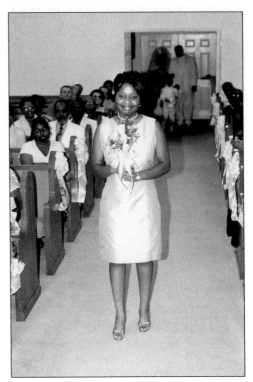

(above, left) Je'ohne Hillman, eldest daughter of John and Mamie Hillman, comes down the aisle. (Courtesy of Mamie Hillman.) *(above, right)* Lea Hillman, youngest daughter of John and Mamie Hillman, comes down the aisle. (Courtesy of Mamie Hillman.)

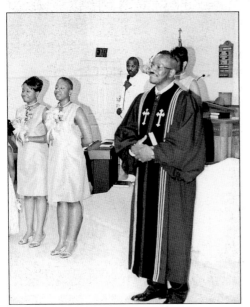 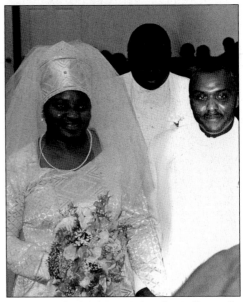

(above, left) Pastor Herman Laguines awaits the bride. In the background, John Hillman Sr. sings "Unforgettable." (Courtesy of Mamie Hillman.) *(above, right)* Finally, the couple arrives at the altar and both are ready to repeat their vows. (Courtesy of Mamie Hillman.)

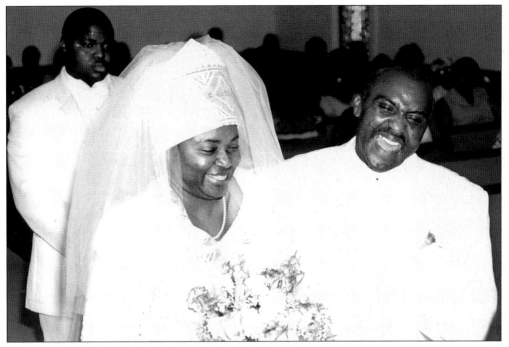

John and Mamie Hillman have created another wonderful memory, sharing a precious moment with family and friends. (Courtesy of Mamie Hillman.)

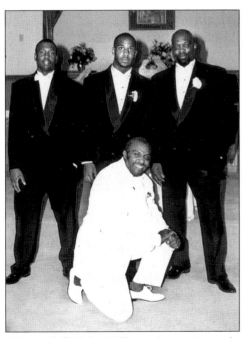

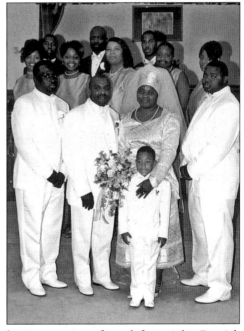

(above, left) John Hillman Sr. is pictured with his groomsmen, from left to right, Derrick Robinson, Justin Taylor, and Leonard Hillman. (Courtesy of Mamie Hillman.) *(above, right)* John and Mamie Hillman are pictured with all the participants from the 25th wedding celebration. (Courtesy of Mamie Hillman.)

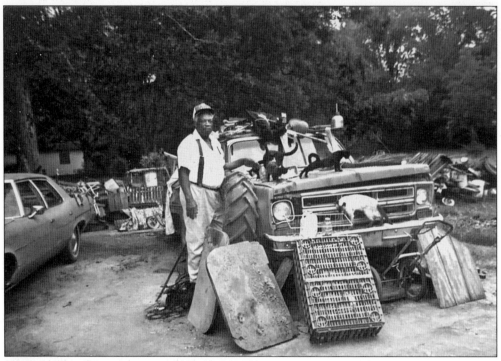

Mr. James Jones Sr. organizes the iron works that he has collected in his yard. (Courtesy of Lucille Tyson.)

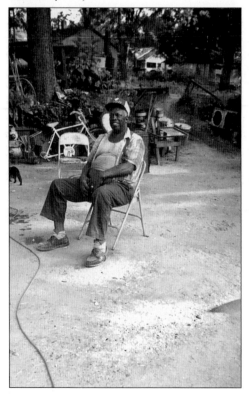

James Jones Sr. rests after a long, busy day in his backyard. (Courtesy of Lucille Tyson.)

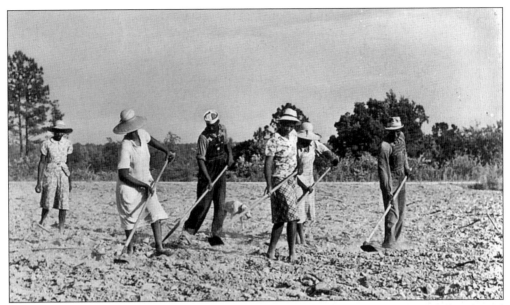

When cotton was king in Greene County, many of our family members hoed and picked cotton for a living. They did this locally as well as rode buses to other counties and did the same to make a living for their families. This mid-1900s photograph was taken of a cotton field in the White Plains, Georgia area. Sometimes entire families worked in the cotton field together. (Courtesy Georgia Division of Archives and History, Office of the Secretary of the State.)

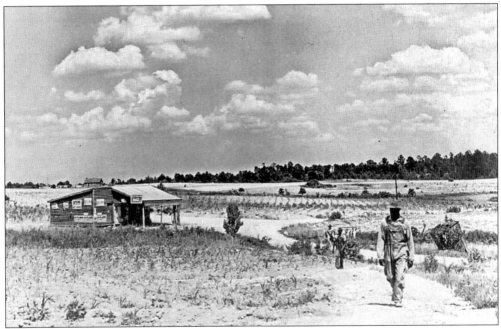

A farmer walks home from a local store at Mosquito Crossing community near Veazey sometime in the mid–1900s. (Courtesy Georgia Division of Archives and History, Office of the Secretary of the State.)

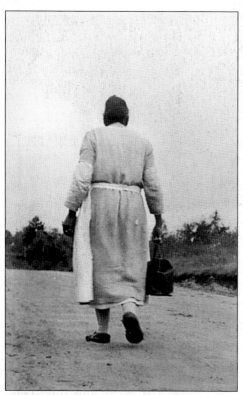

Lucy Russell, a local midwife in Siloam, Georgia, travels down the road with her supplies to deliver a baby. Midwives were a very active part of the medical community from the early 1920s throughout the 1950s in rural communities. (Courtesy Georgia Division of Archives and History, Office of the Secretary of the State.)

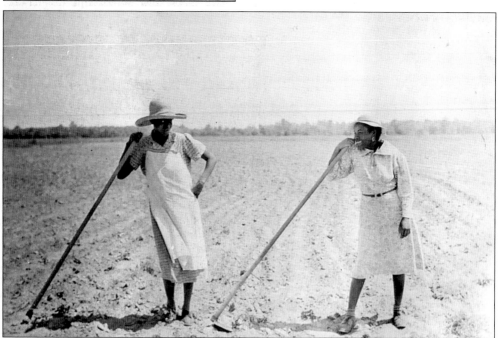

Carrie and Mattie Miller rest on hoe handles after working in the field at Gray Land Road in Greene County, Georgia. (Courtesy Georgia Division of Archives and History, Office of the Secretary of the State.)

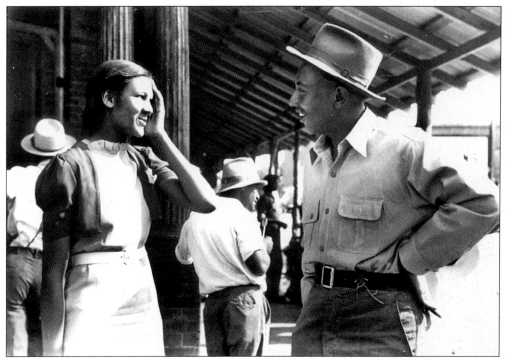

An unidentified woman and man discuss plans for the weekend in downtown White Plains, Georgia, *c*. June 1941. (Courtesy of Hargrett Rare Book and Manuscript Collection, University of Georgia.)

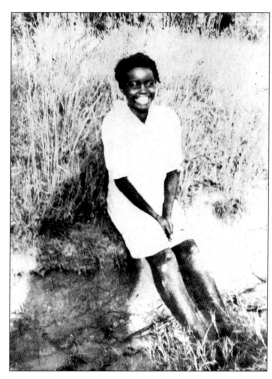

Gusola is the daughter of Mattie Mae Champion of White Plains, Georgia. (Courtesy Georgia Division of Archives and History, Office of the Secretary of the State.)

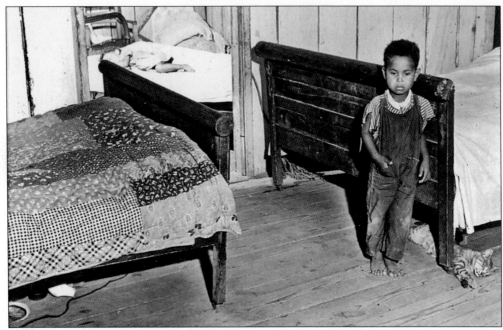

Pictured here is Mrs. Eutha Greene's son, John Moses, *c.* 1940s, in Greene County, Georgia. (Courtesy Georgia Division of Archives and History, Office of the Secretary of the State.)

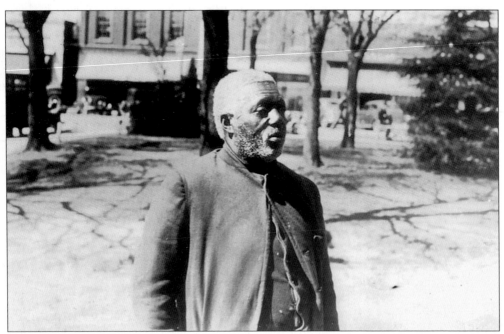

This photographs depicts a former slave in the late 1800s on the Greene County Courthouse lawn, across the street from the Bickers and Goodwin Building on North Main Street in Greensboro, Georgia. (Courtesy of Arthur Raper Collection, Chapel Hill, North Carolina.)